# LUXE knits:
## the ACCESSORIES

# LUXE knits:
## the ACCESSORIES
### Couture Adornments to Knit & Crochet

## Laura ZUKAITE

Photography by Cathrine WESTERGAARD

LARK
CRAFTS

A Division of Sterling Publishing Co., Inc.
New York / London

SENIOR EDITOR
**Valerie Van Arsdale Shrader**

ASSISTANT EDITOR
**Gavin R. Young**

ART DIRECTOR
**Dana Irwin**

ILLUSTRATOR
**Laura Zukaite**

PHOTOGRAPHER
**Cathrine Westergaard**

COVER DESIGNER
**woolypear**

Library of Congress Cataloging-in-Publication Data

Zukaite, Laura.
 Luxe knits : the accessories : couture adornments to knit & crochet / Laura Zukaite. — 1st ed.
   p. cm.
 Includes index.
 ISBN 978-1-60059-585-1 (hc-plc with jacket : alk. paper)
 1. Knitting—Patterns. 2. Crocheting—Patterns. 3. Dress accessories. I. Title.
 TT825.Z853 2010
 746.43'2041—dc22

                              2010000572

10 9 8 7 6 5 4 3 2 1

First Edition

Published by Lark Books, A Division of
Sterling Publishing Co., Inc.
387 Park Avenue South, New York, NY 10016

Text © 2010, Laura Zukaite
Illustrations © 2010, Laura Zukaite
Photography © 2010, Lark Books, A Division of Sterling Publishing Co., Inc.

Distributed in Canada by Sterling Publishing,
c/o Canadian Manda Group, 165 Dufferin Street
Toronto, Ontario, Canada M6K 3H6

Distributed in the United Kingdom by GMC Distribution Services,
Castle Place, 166 High Street, Lewes, East Sussex, England BN7 1XU

Distributed in Australia by Capricorn Link (Australia) Pty Ltd.,
P.O. Box 704, Windsor, NSW 2756 Australia

If you have questions or comments about this book,
please contact:

Lark Books
67 Broadway
Asheville, NC 28801
828-253-0467

Manufactured in China

 ISBN 13: 978-1-60059-585-1

For information about custom editions, special sales, and premium and
 corporate purchases, please contact the Sterling Special Sales Department
 at 800-805-5489 or specialsales@sterlingpub.com.

For information about desk and examination copies available to college and
 university professors, requests must be submitted to academic@larkbooks.com.
 Our complete policy can be found at www.larkbooks.com.

# contents

# introduction

I design for real people. There is nothing more rewarding than seeing your piece "walk" down the street and knowing that you have found that fine line where creativity and functionality merge. I emphasized this idea in my first book, *Luxe Knits:* the end result of my designs has to serve a purpose and be beautiful at the same time. This is especially true of accessories. We like memorable little statement pieces to decorate our lives, so we accessorize to complete our looks—the belt, purse, or gloves often becomes the most important part of the ensemble.

I've always found accessories to be powerful pieces, and I've developed *Luxe Knits: The Accessories* around this idea. You can dress up or dress down depending on how you use a scarf, a pair of wristlets, or a hat, changing your look throughout the day by switching which accessories you wear. You can play it casual for the morning, touch up on some trends during the day, fancy it up in the evening, and add a little glamour for the night…so here is a collection of 28 accessories for the different times and moods of the day.

## We like memorable little statement pieces to decorate our lives.

**The morning is a new beginning.** It is undefined, promising, easy, soft, and relaxed—these are the qualities I wanted to reflect in the Casual Morning Collection by creating pieces that are inviting, comfortable, and effortless to wear. The Long Chunky Scarf (page 30) or the Smocking Leg Warmers (page 14) are very textural and give you that soft and cozy feeling. The Loose Linen Scarf (page 10) and Tonal Triangular Shawl (page 22) are so light and airy that they easily add to the relaxed and uncomplicated mood.

The day is full of action, when you want to stay chic but perhaps still classic. Elegant and fashionable, trendy and memorable, influential, powerful, and enduring—these would be the key words that best define the Trendy Day Collection. The accessories here each make a little statement to impress and garner attention. For example, we all know that some looks never go out of style. You can easily create a timeless look by wearing a Smocking Beret (page 44) or carrying the Smocking Bag (page 40). If you want to turn it up a notch and try something a little more current, the Long Tonal Leg Warmers (page 64) or Lacy Rectangular Scarf (page 56) will definitely do the job.

The evening is the enchanting balance between day and night, when you can dress up your look simply with the addition of a special piece. Playful, feminine, loud, interesting, artistic—this is how I would describe the Early Evening Collection. These accessories can dominate the outfit and serve as statement pieces. For instance, build your look around the Motorcycle Gloves (page 76) and the Motorcycle Rib Headband (page 82), or slip on the Herringbone Bracelet (page 90) for a subtler accent. This collection has the pieces for a perfect transition between work and play.

The night is when you shine! Delicate, sparkly, airy, light, vivid, impressive, flirty, coquettish—these are the elements displayed in the Starry Night Collection. This grouping of projects is all about the feminine details and understated touches that make the accessories special. The Long Silk Gloves (page 104) are distinctive with a bit of glam, but if you want to make a bold statement, try the Corseted Belt (page 108). Go for luxury with the Crocheted Pearl Earrings and Necklace (pages 124 and 128). The nighttime pieces put an exclamation mark on your ensemble.

It is so much fun to play with your accessories throughout the day, changing them to reflect your mood, whether you're feeling casual and maybe a little carefree in the morning or elegant and supremely sophisticated at night. And it is even more fun when they become the key elements of your style, displayed as distinctive adornments that you build an entire look around. I hope that the collections in this book will inspire you to make a special piece for every hour in the day.

CASUAL
MORNING
COLLECTION

## EACH MORNING PROMISES SOMETHING NEW.

Begin the day with pieces that are relaxed and comfortable, easy to wear and easy to enjoy.

# loose linen summer scarf

**Created using lightweight linen yarn,** this scarf has some of the fiber's delightful "crunchiness" yet is still airy and light. A combination of Stockinette and Reverse Stockinette lends it a very interesting texture.

SKILL LEVEL
**Advanced**

FINISHED MEASUREMENTS
**14" x 80"/36cm x 203cm, after blocking, excluding fringe**

YOU WILL NEED

**Claudia Hand Painted Linen Lace** (100% linen; 3.5oz/100g = 540yd/494m): (A) 1 skein, color Antique Jeans; (B) 1 skein, color Country Kitchen; (C) 1 skein, color Deep Blue; (D) 1 skein, color Silver Shimmer—approx 2160yd/1964m of lace weight yarn; 🧶

**Knitting needles:** 4mm (size 6 U.S.) straight needles *or size to obtain gauge*

**Crochet hook for fringe**

**Tapestry needle**

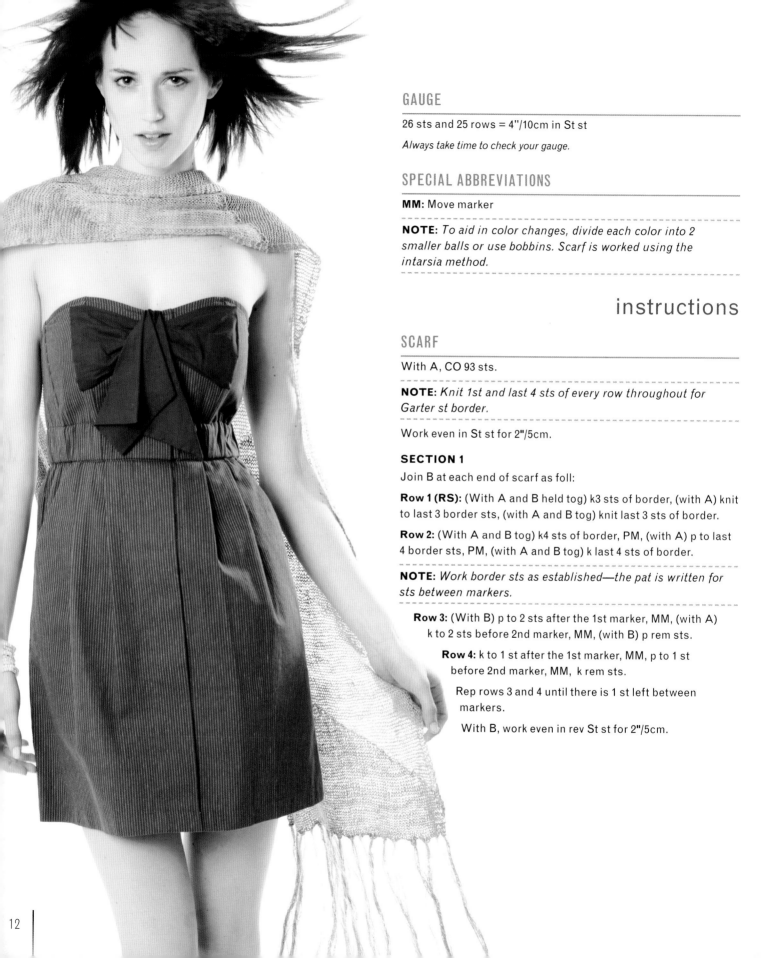

## GAUGE

26 sts and 25 rows = 4"/10cm in St st

*Always take time to check your gauge.*

## SPECIAL ABBREVIATIONS

**MM:** Move marker

**NOTE:** *To aid in color changes, divide each color into 2 smaller balls or use bobbins. Scarf is worked using the intarsia method.*

# instructions

## SCARF

With A, CO 93 sts.

**NOTE:** *Knit 1st and last 4 sts of every row throughout for Garter st border.*

Work even in St st for 2"/5cm.

**SECTION 1**

Join B at each end of scarf as foll:

**Row 1 (RS):** (With A and B held tog) k3 sts of border, (with A) knit to last 3 border sts, (with A and B tog) knit last 3 sts of border.

**Row 2:** (With A and B tog) k4 sts of border, PM, (with A) p to last 4 border sts, PM, (with A and B tog) k last 4 sts of border.

**NOTE:** *Work border sts as established—the pat is written for sts between markers.*

**Row 3:** (With B) p to 2 sts after the 1st marker, MM, (with A) k to 2 sts before 2nd marker, MM, (with B) p rem sts.

**Row 4:** k to 1 st after the 1st marker, MM, p to 1 st before 2nd marker, MM, k rem sts.

Rep rows 3 and 4 until there is 1 st left between markers.

With B, work even in rev St st for 2"/5cm.

## SECTION 2

Join C at each end of scarf as foll:

**Row 1 (RS):** (With B and C tog) k3 sts of border, (with B) p to last 3 border sts, (with B and C tog) k last 3 sts of border.

**Row 2:** (With B and C tog) k4 sts of Border, PM, (with B) knit to last 4 border sts, PM, (with B and C tog) knit last 4 sts of border.

**Row 3:** (With C) k to 2 sts after the 1st marker, MM, (with B) p to 2 sts before the marker, MM, (with C) k rem sts.

**Row 4:** P to 1 st after the 1st marker, MM, k to 1 st before the 2nd marker, MM, p rem sts.

Rep rows 3 and 4 until there is 1 st left between markers.

With C, work even in St st for 2"/5cm.

Rep Section 1, adding D.

Rep Section 2, adding A.

Cont to rep Sections 1 and 2, adding next color as foll: B, C, D, A, B, C. End with 2"/5cm of C.

BO.

## FINISHING

Weave in ends.

Block.

## FRINGE

Cut 24"/61cm long strands of B, C, and D. With crochet hook, attach fringe in groups of 4 strands along end of scarf, alternating colors as foll: C, D, B. Rep on opposite end of scarf.

**E**ffortless and easy to wear, this scarf becomes a perfect casual "throw-on" item to have in your wardrobe. When I started this scarf I wanted to relate it to the Summer Dress from my first book, *Luxe Knits*, so I decided to play with a similar Stockinette/ Reverse-Stockinette pattern in different tones.

# smocking leg warmers

## YOU WILL NEED

**ArtYarns Cashmere Sock** (67% cashmere, 25% wool, 8% nylon; 1.75oz/50g = 160yd/146m): 2 skeins, color #179—approx 255yd/232m of sport weight yarn; **2**

**Small amount of waste yarn in a contrasting color**

**Knitting needles:** 4mm (size 6 U.S.) 16"/41cm circular needle *or size to obtain gauge*

**Tapestry needle**

## SKILL LEVEL
**Intermediate**

## FINISHED MEASUREMENTS
**9"/23cm in circumference, 9½"/24cm long, after smocking**

**This project is perfect for someone** who loves to knit in simple stitches but wants a visually interesting result. Like several other projects in the book, the smocking pattern is not worked as you go, but gathered afterwards.

## GAUGE

22 sts and 22 rows = 4"/10cm in St st, before smocking
*Always take time to check your gauge.*

# instructions

## LEG WARMERS

(Make 2)

CO 80 sts. PM and join in a rnd. Work even in St st until piece measures approx 8½"/22cm from beg.

**Next rnd:** K1, p1, *k1, p2tog; rep from * to end—54 sts.

Work even in k1, p1 rib for 11 rnds more.

BO in pat.

## FINISHING

Weave in ends. Block.

## SMOCKING

### PREPARATION

Mark smocking rows by basting a length of contrasting yarn under the knit sts of the 1st St st rnd, and on every folling 6th rnd on St st portion for a total of 9 marked rnds.

For each "smock," cut a 10"/25cm length of project yarn.

### CREATING THE SMOCKING

Fold 1 length of cut project yarn in half and thread folded end through needle, keeping loop on one side of needle eye.

With RS facing and beg at the 1st st of 1st marked rnd, insert needle under 2nd stitch, *then back up at 8th st (skipping 6 sts). Bring needle back through loop and tighten in a lark's head knot. Insert needle to WS and weave in ends. Skip 8 sts, insert needle under next st as before and rep from * around. For subsequent rnds, beg 1st smock centered between two smocks of prev rnd and work as before.

**Y**oung and chic! Wear them with boots for a fashionable grungy look…or put them on with slippers for a cozy night in.

# earflap hat

**A little touch of classic Aran design** is reflected in the stitch pattern of this project, but it also features a healthy dose of young and hip for a stylish look. A fun piece to make and a great piece to wear when you're off for your morning coffee!

## YOU WILL NEED

**Blue Sky Alpacas Melange** (100% baby alpaca; 1.75oz/ 50g = 110yd/101m): 3 skeins, color Huckleberry #805— approx 330yd/300m of sport weight yarn; **2**

**Knitting needles:** 5mm (size 8 U.S.) 16"/41cm circular needle and set of 5 dpns *or size to obtain gauge*

**Cable needle**

**Tapestry needle**

## SKILL LEVEL
**Advanced**

## FINISHED MEASUREMENTS
**21"/53cm in circumference, after blocking**

## GAUGE

16 sts and 25 rows = 4"/10cm in Seed Stitch with yarn held double

*Always take time to check your gauge.*

## SPECIAL ABBREVIATIONS

**Tw3B:** (twist 3 sts back): Slip next st to cn and hold in back of work, k2, p1 from cn.

**Tw3F:** (twist 3 sts front): Slip next 2 sts to cn and hold in front of work, p1, k2 from cn.

**C4F:** (cable 4 sts front): Slip 2 sts to cn and hold in front of work, k2, k2 from cn.

**C4B:** (cable 4 sts back): Slip 2 sts to cn and hold in back of work, k2, k2 from cn.

**MB (make bobble):** Knit into the front and back of the next stitch twice (4 sts in one stitch), turn; sl 1, p3, turn; sl 1, k3, turn; sl 1, p3, turn; sl 1, k2tog, k1, turn; p3tog, turn and sl this stitch onto the right hand needle.

## PATTERN STITCHES

### SEED STITCH

*(Multiple of 2)*

**Row 1:** *K1, p1; rep from * across.

**Row 2:** *P1, k1; rep from * across.

**Rep rows 1 and 2 for pat.**

### ARAN/BOBBLE

*(Panel of 30 sts)*

**Rnd 1:** P1, *p4, k4; rep from * 3 times, end p5.

**Rnd 2 and all even rnds through 14:** Knit the knit sts and purl the purl sts.

**Rnd 3:** P2, *p2, Tw3B, Tw3F; rep from * 3 times, end p4.

**Rnd 5:** P3, *Tw3B, p2, Tw3F; rep from * 3 times, end p3.

**Rnd 7:** P3, k2, *p1, MB, p1, C4F; rep from * twice, end p1, MB, p1, k2, p3.

**Rnd 9:** P3, *Tw3F, p2, Tw3B; rep from * 3 times, end p3.

**Rnd 11:** P3, *p1, Tw3F, Tw3B, p2; rep from * 3 times, end p2.

**Rnd 13:** P5, *C4B, p1, MB, p1; rep from * twice, end p1, C4B, p5.

**Rep rows 1–14 for pat.**

- - - - - - - - - - - - - - - - - - - - - - - - - - - -
**NOTE:** *Yarn is held double throughout.*
- - - - - - - - - - - - - - - - - - - - - - - - - - - -

# instructions

## EARFLAP

*(Make 2)*

With a double strand of yarn, CO 5 sts.

**Row 1 (WS):** Work in Seed Stitch, CO 2 sts; 7 sts.

**Row 2:** Work in Seed Stitch, CO 2 sts; 9 sts.

**Rows 3 and 4:** Rep rows 1 and 2; 13 sts.

**Row 5:** Work in Seed Stitch, CO 1 st; 14 sts.

**Row 6:** Work in Seed Stitch, CO 1 st; 15 sts.

**Rows 7, 8, and 9:** Work even in Seed Stitch.

**Rows 10 and 11:** Work in Seed Stitch, CO 1 st; 17 sts.

**Rows 12, 13, and 14:** Work even in Seed Stitch.

**Rows 15 and 16:** Work in Seed Stitch, CO 1 st; 19 sts.

**Rows 17, 18, and 19:** Work even in Seed Stitch.

Do not BO. Set aside.

## HAT

CO 30 sts for the front, PM, work in Seed Stitch across 1st ear-flap, CO 19 sts for the back, work in Seed Stitch across 2nd earflap, PM and join in rnd—87 sts.

Work in Aran/Bobble panel pat over front 30 sts, work rest of rnd in Seed Stitch until piece measures 6"/15cm from beg of hat, ending with rnd 10 of Aran/Bobble panel pat.

**Next (dec) rnd:** Work in pat across front, *p2tog, [k1, p1] twice; rep from * to last 3 sts, k1, p2tog—77 sts.

Work even in pat for 3 rnds.

**Next (dec) rnd:** Work in pat across front, *p2tog, k1, p1, k1; rep from * to last 2 sts, k1, p1—68 sts.

Work 1 rnd even.

**Next (dec) rnd:** P2tog, *p2, Tw3B (ssk the 2nd knit and purl sts), Tw3F (k2tog the 1st knit and twisted purl sts); rep from *, end [p2tog] twice, on Seed Stitch section work *p2tog, k1, p1; rep from * to last 2 sts, k1, p1—50 sts.

Work even in pat for 1 rnd.

**Next (dec) rnd:** P2tog, *Tw3B (ssk the 2nd knit and purl sts), Tw3F (k2tog the 1st knit and twisted purl sts); rep from *, end p1, on Seed Stitch section work *p2tog, k1; rep from * to last 2 sts, k1, p1—34 sts.

Work even in pat for 1 rnd.

**Next (dec) rnd:** P1, *C4B (knit the 1st 2 sts tog and the last 2 sts tog); rep from *, end p1, on Seed Stitch section work *p2tog, k1; rep from * to last 2 sts, end p2tog—21 sts.

Work even in pat for 1 rnd.

**Next (dec) rnd:** P1, *k2tog; rep from *, end p1, on Seed Stitch section work *p2tog, k2tog; rep from *, end p1—12 sts.

Work even in pat for 1 rnd.

**Next (dec) rnd:** *P2tog, k2tog; rep from * around—6 sts.

## FINISHING

Cut yarn, leaving a long tail. Pull through rem 6 sts to secure. Weave in ends. Block. Make three 3"/8cm tassels from rem yarn. Hang from earflaps and top of hat with a length of twisted cord.

**V**ery young and so much fun! It's at home in the city or in the backcountry—especially on the ski slope.

# tonal
# triangular
# shawl

**A play with tonal**

**color changes**

combined with

translucent areas

makes this piece

delicate and light,

just like the early

morning.

SKILL LEVEL
**Intermediate**

FINISHED MEASUREMENTS
**64" x 40"/163cm x 102cm,
after blocking**

YOU WILL NEED

**ArtYarns Cashmere 1** (100% cashmere; 1.75oz/50g = 510yd/466m): 1 skein, color #250—approx 510yd/466m of lace weight yarn; **0** (A)

**ArtYarns Cashmere 2** (100% cashmere; 1.75oz/50g = 255yd/233m): 1 skein, color (half strength) #191C—approx 255yd/233m of fingering weight yarn; **1** (B)

**ArtYarns Cashmere 3** (100% cashmere; 1.75oz/50g = 170yd/155m): 3 skeins, color #191C—approx 510yd/466m of light worsted weight yarn; **3** (C)

**Knitting needles:** 4mm (size 6 U.S.) straight needles, 6mm (size 10 U.S.) and 5mm (size 8 U.S.) straight needles *or size to obtain gauge*

**Tapestry needle**

20 sts and 28 rows = 4"/10cm in St st using C and smallest needles
*Always take time to check your gauge.*

## SPECIAL ABBREVIATIONS

**Slk2p:** Slip 1 st as if to knit, k2tog, pass the slipped st over (2 sts dec).

**Ssk3p:** Slip 2 sts as if to knit, k3tog, pass the slipped sts over (4 sts dec).

# instructions

## SCARF

With largest needles and A, CO 257 sts.

- - - - - - - - - - - - - - - - - - - - - - - - - - - - - - - - - - - -

**NOTE:** *Slip 1st st of every row throughout.*

- - - - - - - - - - - - - - - - - - - - - - - - - - - - - - - - - - - -

**Row 1 (WS):** Purl.

**Row 2:** Knit.

**Row 3:** Purl.

**Row 4 (RS):** Mark center stitch and knit to 1 st before marked st, Slk2p, knit to end—255 sts.

**Row 5:** Purl.

Work last 2 rows 3 more times—249 sts.

**Rep rows 4 and 5, changing color as foll:** 1 row B, 2 rows A, 2 rows B, 1 row A—243 sts.

Change to medium size needles and B. Rep rows 4 and 5 five times—233 sts.

Rep rows 4 and 5, changing color as foll: 1 row C, 2 rows B, 2 rows C, 1 row B—227 sts.

Change to smallest needles and C. Rep rows 4 and 5 five times—217 sts.

**Next row (RS):** Knit to 2 sts before marked center st, Ssk3p, knit to end—213 sts.

**Next row:** Purl.

Rep last 2 rows 45 times—33 sts.

**Next row (RS):** Knit to 2 sts before marked st, Ssk3p, knit to end—29 sts.

**Next row:** Purl to 1 st before marked st, p3tog, purl to end—27 sts.

Repeat last 2 rows four more times—3 sts.

**Next row:** Slip 1 stitch, k2tog, psso. Fasten off.

## FINISHING

Weave in ends. Block to measurements.

**T**his shawl's tonal transition in both weight and color is best displayed when effortlessly draped, so let it fall gracefully across your body. This project utilizes one of my favorite techniques.

# multicolor leather bracelet

**Created from strips of leather lace**, this project is very fun and quick to make. All you need are eight different colors of leather lace to combine any way you like.

SKILL LEVEL
**Beginner**

FINISHED MEASUREMENTS
**3¼" x 6½"/8cm x 17cm, blocked, not including fringe**

YOU WILL NEED

⅛" **leather lace,** 4yds/4m in color peach (A)

⅛" **leather lace,** 1yd/1m in following colors: (B) medium brown, (C) caramel brown, (D) olive, (E) camel, (F) brown, (G) red, (H) dark brown

**Knitting needles:** 6mm (size 10 U.S.) straight needles *or size to obtain gauge*

12 sts and 6 rows = 4"/10cm in Garter st, after blocking
*Always take time to check your gauge.*

## instructions

### BRACELET

**NOTE:** *On all rows, leave a 6"/15cm tail on each end for ties.*

With A, CO 20 sts. Cut yarn, turn.

**Next row:** With A, knit. Cut yarn, turn.

Rep last row with each color in sequence: B, C, D, E, F, G, H, A.

With A, BO.

### FINISHING

Knot ties as foll:

Tie beg 2 strands of A tog in an overhand knot, tie rem tails
in groups of 3 strands (4 knots total). Rep on other side, beg
with 2 strands of A. Block lightly to size. To fasten, thread tails
through space above knots on opposite side.

**V**ery trendy...and very easy to make!
This design would also look fabulous in a
single color of leather. Feel free to make
the cuff as tall as you like to achieve a
bolder statement.

# long chunky scarf

**This scarf has very defined stitches that reveal its beautiful texture.** Soft and cozy in alpaca and merino yarn, this scarf is a great addition to anyone's wardrobe.

SKILL LEVEL
**Intermediate**

FINISHED MEASUREMENTS
**14" x 86"/36cm x 218cm, after blocking, excluding fringe**

YOU WILL NEED

Blue Sky Alpacas Bulky (50% alpaca, 50% wool; 3.5oz/100g = 45yd/41m): 10 skeins, color Jasmine #1213—approx 450yd/411m of super bulky weight yarn; (6)

Knitting needles: 12mm (size 17 U.S.) *or size to obtain gauge*

Tapestry needle

Crochet hook for fringe

## GAUGE

6½ sts and 10 rows = 4"/10cm in Trellis pat, before blocking
*Always take time to check your gauge.*

## SPECIAL ABBREVIATIONS

**RTw (right twist):** Sl 1 st purlwise wyib, drop next st off the needle to front of work, slip same purl st back to LH needle, pick up dropped st and knit it, p1.

**LTw (left twist):** Drop next st off the needle to front of work, p1, pick up dropped st and knit it.

## PATTERN STITCH

**TRELLIS**
(Multiple of 8 + 2)

**Rows 1 and 3 (RS):** P1, *p3, k2, p3; rep from * across, end p1.

**Row 2 and all WS rows:** K the knit sts and slip the purl sts wyif.

**Row 5:** P1, *p2, RTw, LTw, p2; rep from * across, end p1.

**Row 7:** P1, *p1, RTw, p2, LTw, p1; rep from * across, end p1.

**Row 9:** P1, *RTw, p4, LTw; rep from * across, end p1.

**Rows 11 and 13:** P1, *k1, p6, k1; rep from * across, end p1.

**Row 15:** P1, *LTw, p4, RTw; rep from * across, end p1.

**Row 17:** P1, *p1, LTw, p2, RTw, p1; rep from * across, end p1.

**Row 19:** P1, *p2, LTw, RTw, p2; rep from * across, end p1.

**Row 20:** Rep row 2.

Rep rows 1–20 for pat.

# instructions

## SCARF

CO 28 sts.

**NOTE:** *There are two extra edge sts — always slip the 1st and knit the last st on each row.*

Work in Trellis pat on center 26 sts until piece measures approx 86"/218cm.
BO.

## FINISHING

Weave in ends. Block.

## FRINGE

Cut 52 pieces of 26"/66cm long yarn.

Using crochet hook, fold 2 strands in half and attach to end of scarf. Rep for rem fringe, for a total of 13 times on each end.

**B**ig and chunky! Make a bold fashion statement by wrapping it around your neck multiple times as if you are trying to cover yourself in it.

# loose
# linen cowl

**A cabled cowl is a great**

**summer accessory.**

Worked in the round, this

seamless piece is shaped

within the cable pattern.

SKILL LEVEL
**Advanced**

FINISHED MEASUREMENTS
**24"/61cm in
circumference at
top, 45"/114cm
in circumference
at bottom,
12½"/32cm long**

YOU WILL NEED

**Claudia Hand Painted Linen**
(100% linen; 3.5oz/100g =
270yd/247m): 2 skeins, color
Silver Shimmer—approx
540yd/494m of sport weight yarn;

**Knitting needles:** 4.5mm (size 7
U.S.) 24"/61 cm circular needle
*or size to obtain gauge*

**Cable needle**

**Tapestry needle**

## GAUGE

24 sts and 22 rnds = 4"/10cm in Twisty Cable pat

*Always take time to check your gauge.*

## SPECIAL ABBREVIATIONS

**C4B (cable 4 sts back):** Slip 2 sts to cn and hold in back of work, k2, k2 from cn.

**Tw3B (twist 3 sts back):** Slip 1 st to cn and hold in back of work, k2, p1 from cn.

**Tw4F (twist 4 sts front):** Slip 2 sts to cn and hold in front of work, p2, k2 from cn.

**Tw4B (twist 4 sts back):** Slip 2 sts to cn and hold in back of work, k2, p2 from cn.

**Tw3F (twist 3 sts front):** Slip 2 sts to cn and hold in front of work, p1, k2 from cn.

**C4F (cable 4 sts front):** Slip 2 sts to cn and hold in front of work, k2, k2 from cn.

**C2B (cable 2 sts back):** Slip 1 st to cn and hold in back of work, k1, k1 from cn.

**Tw2F (twist 2 sts front):** Slip 1 st to cn and hold in front of work, p1, k1 from cn.

**Tw2B (twist 2 sts back):** Slip 1 st to cn and hold in back of work, k1, p1 from cn.

**C2F (cable 2 sts front):** Slip 1 st to cn and hold in front of work, k1, k1 from cn.

## PATTERN STITCH

### TWISTY CABLE

(Panel of 24 sts)

**Rnd 1:** P2, C4B, [p4, C4B] twice, p2.

**Rnd 2:** P2, k4, [p4, k4], twice, p2.

**Rnd 3:** P1, Tw3B, [Tw4F, Tw4B] twice, Tw3F, p1.

**Rnd 4:** P1, k2, p3, k4, p4, k4, p3, k2, p1.

**Rnd 5:** Tw3B, p3, C4F, p4, C4F, p3, Tw3F.

**Rnd 6:** K2, p4, [k4, p4] twice, k2.

**Rnd 7:** K2, p3, Tw3B, Tw4F, Tw4B, Tw3F, p3, k2.

**Rnd 8:** [K2, p3] twice, k4, [p3, k2] twice.

**Rnd 9:** [K2, p3] twice, C4B, [p3, k2] twice.

**Rnd 10:** Rep row 8.

**Rnd 11:** K2, p3, Tw3F, Tw4B, Tw4F, Tw3B, p3, k2.

**Rnd 12:** Rep rnd 6.

**Rnd 13:** Tw3F, p3, C4F, p4, C4F, p3, Tw3B.

**Rnd 14:** Rep rnd 4.

**Rnd 15:** P1, Tw3F, [Tw4B, Tw4F] twice, Tw3B, p1.

**Rnd 16:** Rep rnd 2.

Rep rnds 1–16 for pat.

# instructions

## COWL

CO 270 sts.

Starting with rnd 1 of Twisty Cable panel, work as foll:

*P6, work Twisty Cable panel over next 24 sts; rep from * around.

Cont through rnd 15.

**Rnd 16:** *P2tog, p2, p2tog, work Twisty Cable panel over the next 24 sts; rep from * around—252 sts.

Cont as foll:

*P4, work Twisty Cable panel over next 24 sts; rep from * around.

Cont through rnd 7.

**Rnd 8:** *P2tog, p2tog, work Twisty Cable panel over next 24 sts; rep from * around—234 sts.

Cont as follows:

*P2, work Twisty Cable panel over next 24 sts; rep from * around.

Cont through rnd 15.

**Rnd 16:** *P2tog, work Twisty Cable panel over next 24 sts; rep from * around—225 sts.

Cont as foll:

*P1, work Twisty Cable panel over next 24 sts; rep from * around.

Cont through rnd 7.

**Rnd 8:** *P1, k2tog, p1, p2tog, k2tog, p1, p2tog, [k2tog] twice, p1, p2tog, k2tog, p1, p2tog, k2tog; rep from * around—135 sts.

**Rnd 9:** *P1, [k1, p2] twice, C2B, [p2, k1] twice; rep from * around.

**Rnd 10:** *P1, [k1, p2] twice, k2, [p2, k1] twice; rep from * around.

**Rnd 11:** *P1, k1, p2, [Tw2F, Tw2B] twice, p2, k1; rep from * around.

**Rnd 12:** *P1, k1, p3, k2, p2, k2, p3, k1; rep from * around.

**Rnd 13:** *P1, Tw2F, p2, C2F, p2, C2F, p2, Tw2B; rep from * around.

**Rnd 14:** *P2, k1, [p2, k2] twice, p2, k1, p1; rep from * around.

**Rnd 15:** *P2, [Tw2F, Tw2B] 3 times, p1; rep from * around.

**Rnd 16:** *P1, [p2, k2] 3 times, p2; rep from * around.

**Rnd 17:** *P3, C2B, [p2, C2B] twice, p2; rep from * around.

**Rnd 18:** Rep rnd 16.

**Rnd 19:** *P2, [Tw2B, Tw2F] 3 times, p1; rep from * around.

**Rnd 20:** *P2, k1, [p2, k2] twice, p2, k1, p1; rep from * around.

**Rnd 21:** *P1, Tw2B, p2, C2F, p2, C2F, p2, Tw2F; rep from * around.

**Rnd 22:** *P1, k1, p3, k2, p2, k2, p3, k1; rep from * around.

**Rnd 23:** *P1, k1, p2, [Tw2B, Tw2F] twice, p2, k1; rep from * around.

**Rnd 24:** *P1, k1, p2, k1, p2, k2, p2, k1, p2, k1; rep from * around.

Work rnds 9–24 until piece measures 12½"/32cm from beg.

BO.

## FINISHING

Weave in ends. Block.

**A**lthough this piece is made of linen, you can achieve a completely different look if you use another fiber: Wool will give you more bounce, silk will give it a soft drape and a less casual sheen, and cotton will eliminate the crunchiness. So feel free to experiment and re-invent this cowl.

# TRENDY
## DAY
# COLLECTION

**THE DAY IS ALWAYS BUSY.** But staying stylish and chic is simple when you add unique accessories that are elegant yet still fashion-forward.

# smocking bag

## YOU WILL NEED

**Claudia Hand Painted Linen** (100% linen; 3.5oz/100g = 270yd/246m): 2 skeins, color Chocolate—approx 540yd/492m of sport weight yarn; **2**

**Small amount of waste yarn in a contrasting color**

**Knitting needles:** 4.5mm (size 7 U.S.) straight needles and set of 2 dpns *or size to obtain gauge*

**Crochet hook:** 4.25mm (size G or H U.S.)

**Lining fabric (optional)**

**Tapestry needle**

## SKILL LEVEL
**Intermediate**

## FINISHED MEASUREMENTS
**11½" x 19"/29cm x 48cm, after smocking**

**Knit one row, purl one row…**and then gather this basic fabric into a fancy smocking pattern. This simple technique produces a sophisticated accessory for your chic daytime look.

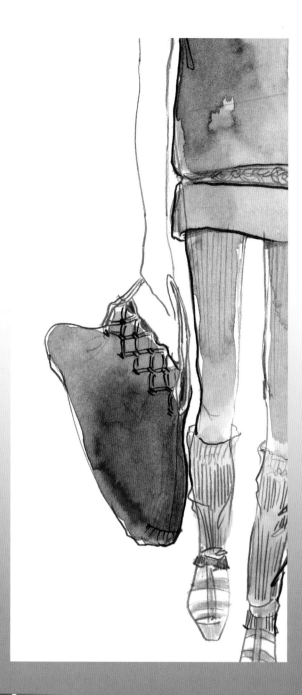

I love bags that do not have a definitive shape. This piece will transform itself depending on which fiber you use. Make it out of linen and you will get a wrinkly summer look...make it out of silk and you can create a dressier version.

## GAUGE

24 sts and 28 rows = 4"/10cm in St st, before smocking
*Always take time to check your gauge.*

# instructions

## BAG

CO 92 sts.

Work in St st for 15"/38cm.

BO 12 sts at beg of next 2 rows—68 sts. Work even for 8"/20cm more for bottom of bag.

CO 12 sts at beg of next 2 rows—92 sts.

Work in St st for 15"/38cm more.

BO loosely.

## FINISHING

Block. Sew side seams, leaving top 8"/20cm of side edges open (do not sew bottom of bag into side seams). Gather bag bottom and sew in place, easing in fullness. Weave in ends.

## SMOCKING

### PREPARATION

Mark smocking rows by basting a length of contrasting yarn under knit sts of row 4 (counting down from top edge of bag) and on every following 6th row, for a total of 4 rows (on front and back of bag).

For each "smock," cut a 10"/25cm length of project yarn.

### CREATING THE SMOCKING

Fold 1 length of cut project yarn in half and thread folded end through needle, keeping loop on one side of needle eye.

With RS facing and beg at the 1st st of the 1st marked row, insert needle under 2nd stitch, *then back up at 6th st (skipping 4 sts). Bring needle back through loop and tighten in a lark's head knot. Insert needle to WS and weave in ends. Skip 6 sts, insert needle under next st as before and rep from * across. For next row, work a smock centered between smocks of prev row. Rep these two smocking rows for pat.

With crochet hook, work 1 row of sc and top edges of bag, firming top edge to prevent smocking from flaring. Fasten off. Weave in ends.

Line bag if desired.

## HANDLES AND SIDE TRIM

With dpns and starting at the bottom of the right side opening on bag front, CO 4 sts. *Pick up and knit 1 st from the edge of the bag. Slide all 5 sts to opposite end of needle, k3, k2tog; rep from * to top edge of bag.

**Work handle on rem 4 sts as foll:** *Slide all 4 sts to opposite end of needle, k4; rep from * until cord measures 30"/76cm. Join handle to left side edge of bag front and work down side as before. BO. Rep on back of bag. Weave in ends.

# smocking beret

**Worked on a circular needle in Stockinette stitch,** this hat has a surprise in store— the flat pattern is transformed after knitting and becomes a textural treat to enjoy throughout the day.

## YOU WILL NEED

**ArtYarns Cashmere 2** (100% cashmere; 1.75oz/50g = 255yd/233m): 1 skein, color #282—approx 255yd/232m of fingering weight yarn; **1**

Small amount of waste yarn in a contrasting color

**Knitting needles:** 4.5mm (size 7 U.S.) 16"/41cm circular needle and set of 5 dpns *or size to obtain gauge*

Tapestry needle

## SKILL LEVEL
**Experienced**

## FINISHED MEASUREMENTS
**20"/51cm in circumference, after smocking**

## GAUGE

26 sts and 26 rows = 4"/10cm in Stockinette stitch, before smocking

*Always take time to check your gauge.*

# instructions

## BRIM

With circular needle, CO 102 sts. PM and join in rnd.

**Rnds 1 and 2:** Knit.

**Rnd 3:** Purl.

**Rnds 4 and 5:** Knit.

**Rnd 6:** Pick up corresponding st of CO row and k2tog with every stitch on the needle to create a folded hem.

**Next (inc) rnd:** K3, *k1, M1; rep from * to last 3 sts, k3—150 sts. Work even in St st until piece measures 4½"/11cm from beg.

## SHAPE CROWN

**NOTE:** *Change to dpns when needed.*

- - - - - - - - - - - - - - - - - - - - - - - - - - - - -

**Rnd 1:** *K2tog, k13; rep from * to end of rnd—140 sts.

**Rnds 2, 3, and 4:** Knit.

**Rnd 5:** *K2tog, k12; rep from * to end of rnd—130 sts.

**Rnds 6, 7, and 8:** Knit.

**Rnd 9:** *K2tog, k11; rep from * to end of rnd—120 sts.

**Rnds 10, 11, and 12:** Knit.

**Rnd 13:** *K2tog, k10; rep from * to end of rnd—110 sts.

**Next rnd:** Knit.

**Next rnd:** Dec as before, working 1 less st between decreases each time as established.

Rep last 2 rnds until 10 sts rem.

## FINISHING

Cut yarn, leaving a long tail. Pull through rem 10 sts to secure. Weave in ends. Block.

## SMOCKING BORDER

### PREPARATION

Mark smocking rows by basting a length of contrasting yarn under the knit sts of rnd 1, right above folded hem and on every following 6th rnd for a total of 4 marked rnds.

For each "smock," cut a 10"/25cm length of project yarn.

### CREATING THE SMOCKING

Fold 1 length of cut project yarn in half and thread folded end through needle, keeping loop on one side of needle eye.

With RS facing and beg at the 1st st of 1st marked rnd, insert needle under 2nd stitch, *then back up at the 6th st (skipping 4 sts). Bring needle back through loop and tighten in a lark's head knot. Insert needle to the WS and weave in ends. Skip 6 sts, insert needle under the next st as before and rep from * around. For subsequent rnds, beg 1st smock centered between two smocks of the prev rnd and work as before.

**A** classic beret with a smocking texture for a proper preppy look. Wear it with a wool blazer and a pair of jeans for a traditional ensemble.

# cable belt

**Worked in a cable pattern,** this tie-on linen belt is a great textural piece to accentuate a simple outfit.

## SKILL LEVEL
**Advanced**

## FINISHED MEASUREMENTS
**2½" x 34"/6cm x 86cm, blocked, not including ties (or to length desired)**

## YOU WILL NEED

**Claudia Hand Painted Linen** (100% linen; 3.5oz/100g = 270yd/247m): 1 skein, color Woodland Moss—approx 270yd/247m of sport weight yarn; **2**

**Knitting needles:** 4.5mm (size 7 U.S.) straight needles *or size to obtain gauge*

**Cable needle**

**Tapestry needle**

**Crochet hook for fringe**

## GAUGE

26 sts = 2¼"/6cm in pat

28 rows = 3½"/9cm in pat

*Always take time to check your gauge.*

## SPECIAL ABBREVIATIONS

**C6B (cable 6 sts back):** Slip 3 sts to cn and hold in back of work, k3, k3 from cn.

**C6F (cable 6 sts front):** Slip 3 sts to cn and hold in front of work, k3, k3 from cn.

**Tw5L (twist 5 sts to the left):** Slip 3 next sts to cn and hold in front of work, p2, k3 from cn.

**Tw5R (twist 5 sts to the right):** Slip 2 next sts to cn and hold in back of work, k3, p2 from cn.

## PATTERN STITCHES

### CABLE PANEL

*Panel of 26 sts*

**Row 1 (RS):** K6, [p4, k6] twice.

**Row 2:** P6, [k4, p6] twice.

**Row 3:** C6B, [P4, C6B] twice.

**Row 4:** Rep row 2.

**Row 5 to 8:** Rep rows 5–8.

**Row 9:** K3, Tw5L, p2, k6, p2, Tw5R, k3.

**Row 10:** [P3, k2] twice, p6, [k2, p3] twice.

**Row 11:** [Tw5L] twice, k6, [Tw5R] twice.

**Row 12:** K2, p3, k2, p12, k2, p3, k2.

**Row 13:** P2, Tw5L, [C6F] twice, Tw5R, p2.

**Row 14:** K4, p18, k4.

**Row 15:** P4, [C6B] 3 times, p4.

**Row 16:** K4, p18, k4.

**Row 17:** P2, Tw5R, [C6F] twice, Tw5L, p2.

**Row 18:** Rep row 12.

**Row 19:** [Tw5R] twice, k6, [Tw5L] twice.

**Row 20:** Rep row 10.

**Row 21:** K3, Tw5R, p2, k6, p2, Tw5L, k3.

**Rows 22 to 28:** Rep rows 2–8.

Rep Rows 1–28 for pat.

# instructions

## BELT

CO 20 sts.

**Row 1 (WS):** Purl.

**Row 2:** Sl 1, [C6F] 3 times, k1, CO 2 sts, turn.

**Row 3:** Sl 1, k2, p18, k1, CO 2 sts, turn—24 sts.

**Row 4:** Sl 1, Tw5R, [C6F] twice, Tw5L, p1, CO 3 sts, turn.

**Row 5:** Sl 1, k3, p3, k2, p12, k2, p3, k1, CO 3 sts, turn—30 sts.

**Row 6:** Sl 1, p1, [Tw5R] twice, k6, [Tw5L] twice, p2.

**Row 7:** K2, PM, work row 20 of Cable Panel, PM, k2.

**Row 8:** P2, slip marker, work row 21 of Cable Panel, slip marker, p2.

**NOTE:** *Continue working as set, working Cable Panel between the markers until desired length is reached, ending with row 12 of Cable Panel. Finish as follows:*

**Row 13:** BO 3 sts, Tw5L, [C6F] twice, Tw5R, p4.

**Row 14:** BO 3 sts, k2, p18, k3.

**Row 15:** BO 2 sts, [C6B] 3 times.

**Row 16:** BO 2 sts, p19.

BO.

## FINISHING

Weave in ends. Cut twenty 40"/102cm long pieces of yarn. With a crochet hook, fold 2 strands in half over hook and join to end of belt; rep 4 more times. Rep on opposite side. Tie each group of 2 strands of fringe in an overhand knot. Approx 1"/2.5cm below these knots, tie all fringe on each side tog in an overhand knot.

**B**elts are fun and functional accents. The Cable Belt adds some textural pattern to your outfit, and the dangling fringe creates playful movement.

**A change in color
tones and yarn weights**
makes the fabric very
airy and delicate, but
warm enough to keep
you cozy throughout
a fall afternoon. A
design twist creates the
interesting texture.

# tonal
# arm
# warmers

**SKILL LEVEL**
**Intermediate**

**FINISHED MEASUREMENTS**
**7"/18cm in**
**circumference,**
**9½"/24cm long,**
**after smocking**

## YOU WILL NEED

**ArtYarns Cashmere 3** (100% cashmere; 1.75oz/50g = 170yd/155m): 1 skein, color #283—approx 170yd/155m of light worsted weight yarn; **3** (A)

**ArtYarns Cashmere 2** (100% cashmere; 1.75oz/50g = 255yd/233m): 1 skein, color #282—approx 255yd/232m of fingering weight yarn; **1** (B)

**ArtYarns Cashmere 1** (100% cashmere; 1.75oz/50g = 510yd/466m): 1 skein, color #233—approx 510yd/466m of lace weight yarn; **0** (C)

**Small amount of waste yarn in a contrasting color**

**Knitting needles:** 4mm (size 6 U.S) set of 5 dpns, 5mm (size 8 U.S.) set of 5 dpns, and 5.5mm (size 9 U.S.) set of 5 dpns *or size to obtain gauge*

**Tapestry needle**

## GAUGE

22 sts and 28 rows = 4"/10cm in St st using C and smallest needles, before smocking
*Always take time to check your gauge.*

# instructions

## ARM WARMERS

(Make 2)

With A and largest needles, CO 64 sts. PM and join in rnd.

Work even in St st for 14 rnds. Change to medium size needles. Work 1 rnd in B, 2 rnds in A, 2 rnds in B, and 1 rnd in A.

Change to B and work even in St st for 14 rnds. Change to smallest needles. Work 1 rnd in C, 2 rnds in B, 2 rnds in C, and 1 rnd in B. Change to C and work even in St st until piece measures approx 9"/23cm from beg. Next rnd: K1, p1, *k1, p2tog; rep from * to last 2 sts, k1, p1—44 sts.

Work even in k1, p1 rib for 10 rnds.

BO in pat.

## FINISHING

Block.

## SMOCKING

### PREPARATION
Mark smocking rows by basting a length of contrasting yarn under the knit sts of 1st St st rnd, and on every following 6th rnd on St st portion for a total of 11 marked rnds.

For each "smock," cut a 10"/25cm length of project yarn.

### CREATING THE SMOCKING
Fold 1 length of cut project yarn in half and thread folded end through needle, keeping loop on one side of needle eye.

With RS facing and beg at 1st st of 1st marked rnd, insert needle under 2nd stitch, *then back up at 8th st (skipping 6 sts). Bring needle back through loop and tighten in a lark's head knot. Insert needle to WS and weave in ends. Skip 8 sts, insert needle under next st as before and rep from * around. For subsequent rnds, beg 1st smock centered between two smocks of prev rnd and work as before.

**A**rm warmers are always a fun accessory. They can blend in with your outfit for a more conservative look… or they can contrast it to make the mood more playful. They also pair well with the Smocking Beret on page 44.

**Created in a fine silk yarn,** this little shawl has beautiful drape. The lacy pattern is perfect for this very girly accessory.

# lacy
# rectangular
# scarf

**SKILL LEVEL**
**Advanced**

**FINISHED
MEASUREMENTS**
**33" x 33"/84cm x
84cm after blocking,
excluding fringe**

## YOU WILL NEED

**Claudia Hand Painted Silk Lace**
(100% silk; 3.5oz/100g =
1100yd/1006m): 1 skein, color
marigold—approx 1100yd/1006m
of lace weight yarn;

**Knitting needles:** 4mm (size 6
U.S.) straight needles *or size
to obtain gauge*

**Crochet hook for fringe**

**Tapestry needle**

The key to wearing this piece is to make it look effortless. Overlay the lacy textures one on top of the other so that they create an unexpected pattern. You can wear this piece as a scarf or as a shawl—just play with it.

GAUGE

20 sts and 32 rows = 4"/10cm in Lace pat, before blocking
*Always take time to check your gauge.*

## PATTERN STITCHES

### LACE

*(Multiple of 24 + 2)*

**Row 1 and all other WS rows:** Purl, working (k1, p1) into each double yo of previous row.

**Row 2:** K1, *yo, [k2tog] twice, yo, k2, k2tog, yo, k2, ssk, [yo] twice, k2tog, k2, yo, ssk, k2, yo, [ssk] twice, yo; rep from * across, end k1.

**Row 4:** K1, *yo, k3tog, yo, [k2, k2tog, yo] twice, k2, [yo, ssk, k2] twice, yo, sl 1-k2tog-psso, yo; rep from * across, end k1.

**Row 6:** K1, *yo, k2tog, [k2, k2tog, yo] twice, ssk, [yo] twice, k2tog, [yo, ssk, k2] twice, ssk, yo; rep from * across, end k1.

**Row 8:** K1, *yo, k2tog, k1, k2tog, yo, k2, k2tog, yo, k1, ssk, [yo] twice, k2tog, k1, yo, ssk, k2, yo, ssk, k1, ssk, yo; rep from * across, end k1.

Rep rows 1–8 for pat.

# instructions

## SCARF

CO 148 sts.

- - - - - - - - - - - - - - - - - - - - - - - - - - - - -
**NOTE:** *There are 2 extra edge sts — always slip the 1st and knit the last st of each row throughout.*
- - - - - - - - - - - - - - - - - - - - - - - - - - - - -

Work in Lace pat on center 146 sts until piece measures 33"/84cm from beg. BO in pat.

## FINISHING

Weave in ends. Block to measurements.

## FRINGE

Cut strands of yarn 18"/46cm long. With crochet hook, attach fringe in groups of 4 strands evenly along end of scarf; approx 30 groups of fringe. If desired, knot fringe in pairs approx 2"/5cm from edge using an overhand knot. Rep on opposite end of scarf.

# lightweight linen hat

## YOU WILL NEED

**Claudia Hand Painted Linen Lace**
(100% linen; 3.5oz/100g =
540yd/494m): (A) 1 skein, color
Silver Shimmer; (B) 1 skein,
color Antique Jeans—
approx 1080yd/988m of lace
weight yarn,

**Knitting needles:** 3.25mm
(size 3 U.S.) 16"/41cm circular
needle *or size to obtain gauge*

**Tapestry needle**

**77 crystal beads (optional)**

## SKILL LEVEL
**Advanced**

## FINISHED MEASUREMENTS
**19"/48cm in
circumference**

**This hat is a perfect summer accessory.** Knit in a linen lace yarn, the loose stitches change color and texture, making the hat a fun piece to work.

## GAUGE

30 sts and 32 rows = 4"/10cm in St st

*Always take time to check your gauge.*

## PATTERN STITCHES

**ZIGZAG**

(Multiple of 13)

**Rnds 1–6:** Knit.

**Rnds 7 and 8:** *K12, p1; rep from * around.

**Rnds 9 and 10:** P1, *k10, p3; rep from * around, end k10, p2.

**Rnds 11 and 12:** P2, *k8, p5; rep from * around, end k8, p3.

**Rnds 13 and 14:** P3, *k6, p7; rep from * around, end k6, p4.

**Rnds 15 and 16:** P4, *k4, p9; rep from * around, end k4, p5.

**Rnds 17 and 18:** P5, *k2, p11; rep from * around, end k2, p6.

**Rnds 19–24:** Purl.

**Rnds 25 and 26:** *P12, k1; rep from * around.

**Rnds 27 and 28:** K1, *p10, k3; rep from * around, end p10, k2.

**Rnds 29 and 30:** K2, *p8, k5; rep from * around, end p8, k3.

**Rnds 31 and 32:** K3, *p6, k7; rep from * around, end p6, k4.

**Rnds 33 and 34:** K4, *p4, k9; rep from * around, end p4, k5.

**Rnds 35 and 36:** K5, *p2, k11; rep from * around, end p2, k6.

Rep rnds 1–36 for pat.

# instructions

## HAT

CO 144 sts. Work in k2, p2 rib until piece measures 3"/8cm from beg. Change to Zigzag pat, dec 1 st on the first knit round—143 sts. Work rnds 1–36 twice, then rnds 1–18 once more.

Beg with Rnd 19, shape crown as foll:

**Rnd 19:** P5, *p2tog, p11; rep from * around, end p2tog, p6—132 sts.

**Rnds 20, 22, and 24:** Purl.

**Rnd 21:** P5, *p2tog, p10; rep from * around, end p2tog, p5—121 sts.

**Rnd 23:** P5, *P2tog, p9; rep from * around, end p2tog, p4—110 sts.

Cont as follows:

**Rnd 1:** P5, p2tog, *p2, k1, p5, p2tog; rep from * around; end p2, k1—99 sts.

**Rnd 2:** *P8, k1; rep from * around.

**Rnd 3:** K1, *P4, p2tog, k3; rep from * around, end p4, p2tog, k2—88 sts.

**Rnd 4:** K1, *p5, k3; rep from * around, end p5, k2.

**Rnd 5:** K2, *p3, k2tog, k3; rep from * around, end p3, k2tog, k1—77 sts.

**Rnd 6:** K2, *p2, k5; rep from * around, end p2, k3.

**Rnd 7:** K4, k2tog, *k5, k2tog; rep from * around, end k1—66 sts.

**Rnd 8 and even rnds through 18:** Knit.

**Rnd 9:** K3, *k2tog, k4; rep from * around, end k2tog, k1—55 sts.

**Rnd 11:** K2, k2tog, *k3, k2tog; rep from * around, end k1—44 sts.

**Rnd 13:** K1, *k2tog, k2; rep from * around, end k2tog, k1—33 sts.

**Rnd 15:** *K2tog, k1; rep from * around—22 sts.

**Rnd 17:** *K2tog; rep from * around—11 sts.

**Rnd 19:** *K2tog; rep from * to last st, k1—6 sts.

## FINISHING

Cut yarn, leaving a long tail. Pull through rem 6 sts to secure. Weave in ends. Block. If desired, sew a crystal bead at each zigzag point.

The greatest part about this hat is the contradiction between the moods. The contrasting elements of casual, crunchy linen and dressy, sparkly crystals make this hat a perfect day item with glowing touches of the night to come.

**Worked in a simple rib pattern,** these leg warmers are a result of creative play with textures and colors, yet the transitions between the different elements remain very subtle.

# long tonal leg warmers

### SKILL LEVEL
**Intermediate**

### FINISHED MEASUREMENTS
**11"/28cm in circumference (stretched), 19½"/50cm long**

## YOU WILL NEED

**ArtYarns Silk Mohair** (60% super kid mohair, 40% silk; 0.88oz/25g = 312yd/285m): 1 skein, color #250—approx 312yd/285m of lace weight yarn; (0) (A)

**ArtYarns Regal Silk** (100% silk; 1.75oz/50g = 163yd/149m): (B) 1 skein, color #275; (C) 1 skein, color #203; (D) 1 skein, color #202—approx 489yd/447m of light worsted weight yarn; (3)

**Knitting needles:** 4mm (size 6 U.S.) set of 5 dpns and 5mm (size 8 U.S) set of 5 dpns *or size to obtain gauge*

**Tapestry needle**

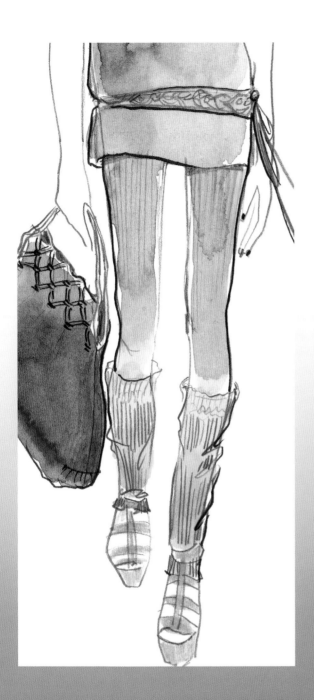

40 sts and 26 rows = 4"/10cm in k1, p1 rib using smaller needles, unstretched

*Always take time to check your gauge.*

# instructions

## LEG WARMERS

With larger needles and A, CO 52 sts. PM and join in rnd. Knit 3 rnds. Change to k1, p1 rib and work even for 20 rnds. Cont in rib pat, work 1 rnd B, 2 rnds A, 2 rnds B, 1 rnd A.

Change to B and work in pat for 20 rnds. Work 1 rnd C, 2 rnds B, 2 rnds C, 1 rnd B.

Change to C and work in pat for 20 rnds.

Change to smaller needles. Work 1 rnd D, 2 rnds C, 2 rnds D, 1 rnd C.

Change to D and work in pat until piece measures 19½"/50cm from beg.

BO loosely in pat.

## FINISHING

Weave in ends.

I decided to make these fun and bright, but with a feminine touch. Since this is meant to be a very youthful accessory, don't be afraid of color.

EARLY
EVENING
COLLECTION

# n

**NOT QUITE DAY, AND NOT YET NIGHT,
THE EVENING IS A TIME OF TRANSITION.**

Choose a special piece to take you
from work to play.

# belted
# purse

**Design meets function!**

**Knit in silk,** this purse
has a dressy look,
while the belt makes
it a very functional
object when worn
around the hips.

SKILL LEVEL
**Advanced**

FINISHED MEASUREMENTS
**8½" x 10"/22cm x 25cm**

YOU WILL NEED

**ArtYarns Regal Silk** (100% silk;
1.75oz/50g = 163yd/149m):
2 skeins, color #274—approx
326yd/298m of light worsted
weight yarn; (3) (A)

**ArtYarns Silk Pearl** (100% silk;
1.75oz/50g = 170yd/155m): 1 skein,
color #274—approx 170yd/155m
of DK weight yarn; (3) (B)

**Knitting needles:** 4mm (size 6 U.S.)
straight needles and 3.75 mm (size
5 U.S.) set of 2 dpns *or size to
obtain gauge*

**Cable needle**

**Stitch holder**

**Tapestry needle**

**Lining fabric (optional)**

**2 D-rings for the belt closure**

**Small crochet hook**

## GAUGE

24 sts and 40 rows = 4"/10cm in Seed Stitch using larger needles
*Always take time to check your gauge.*

## SPECIAL ABBREVIATIONS

**C6B (cable 6 sts back):** Slip 3 sts to cn and hold in back of work, k3, k3 from cn.

**Tw5B(twist 5 sts back):** Slip 2 sts to cn and hold in back of work, k3, p1, k1 from cn.

**Tw5F (twist 5 sts front):** Slip 3 sts to cn and hold in front of work, p1, k1, k3 from cn.

## PATTERN STITCHES

### SEED
(Multiple of 2)

**Row 1:** *K1, p1; rep from * to end.

**Row 2:** *P1, k1; rep from * to end.

### ARAN
(Multiple of 14 + 2)

**Row 1 (RS):** K1, *[p1, k1] twice, k6, [p1, k1] twice; rep from *, end k1.

**Rows 2, 4, and 22:** P1, *[k1, p1] twice, p6, [k1, p1] twice; rep from *, end p1.

**Row 3:** K1, *[p1, k1] twice, C6B, [p1, k1] twice; rep from *, end k1.

**Row 5:** K1, *p1, k1, Tw5B, Tw5F, p1, k1; rep from *, end k1.

**Rows 6 and 8:** P1, *k1, p4, k1, p1, k1, p4, k1, p1; rep from *, end p1.

**Row 7:** K1, *p1, k4, p1, k1, p1, k4, p1, k1; rep from *, end k1.

**Row 9:** K1, *Tw5B, [p1, k1] twice, Tw5F; rep from *, end k1.

**Rows 10, 12, 14, and 16:** P1, *p3, [k1, k1] 4 times, p3; rep from *, end p1.

**Rows 11 and 15:** K4, *[p1, k1] 4 times, C6B; rep from* to last 12 sts, [p1, k1] 4 times, k4.

**Row 13:** K1, *k3, [p1, k1] 4 times, k3; rep from *, end k1.

**Row 17:** K1, *Tw5F, [p1, k1] twice, Tw5B; rep from *, end k1.

**Rows 18 & 20:** P1, *k1, p4, [k1, p1] twice, p3, k1, p1; rep from *, end p1.

**Row 19:** K1, *p1, k4, [p1, k1] twice, k3, p1, k1; rep from *, end k1.

**Row 21:** K1, *p1, k1, Tw5F, Tw5B, p1, k1; rep from *, end k1.

**Row 23:** Rep row 3.

**Row 24:** Rep row 2.

Rep rows 1–24 for pat.

# instructions

## FRONT PANEL

With A and larger needles, CO 74 sts.

**NOTE:** *There are 2 extra edge sts—always slip the 1st st and knit the last st of every row.*

Work in k1, p1 rib for 12 rows.

**Next row:** Sl 1, *k2tog, yo; rep from *, end k1.

Continue working rib for 12 more rows.

Change to Seed Stitch and work evenly in pat for 6 rows.

Dec 1 st at each end of the next row—72 sts.

Cont working evenly as set until Seed Stitch portion measures 3"/8cm.

**On the next (and every following) RS row:** Dec 1 st at each end of row until 58 sts rem.

Dec 1 st at each end of every row until 30 sts rem.

BO.

## BACK PANEL

With A and larger needles, CO 74 sts.

**NOTE:** *There are 2 extra edge sts—always slip 1st st and knit last st of every row.*

Work in k1, p1 rib for 12 rows.

**Next row:** Sl 1, *k2tog, yo; rep from *, end k1.

Cont working in rib for 12 more rows.

**Next row:** M1 by knitting into front and back of every st—148 sts.

Divide the sts as foll: slide every other st onto a holder and leave in front of work to be worked later for flap—74 sts.

Work rem 74 sts in Seed Stitch for 6 rows.

Dec 1 st at each end of the next row—72 sts.

Cont working evenly as set until Seed Stitch portion measures 3"/8cm.

**On the next (and every following) RS row:** Dec 1 st at each end of row until 58 sts rem.

Dec 1 st at each end of every row until 30 sts rem.
BO.

## FLAP

Slide 74 held sts to needle.

**NOTE:** *There are 2 extra edge sts—always slip 1st st and knit last st of every row.*

Work the Aran pat (5 times across row) for 3 repeats (72 rows), then work rows 1–8.

Decrease as foll:

**Row 9 (RS):** Sl 1, k2, Tw5B (except work k3, k2tog), [p1, k1] twice * Tw5B, [p1, k1] twice, Tw5F; rep from *, end Tw5F (except work p2tog, k3), k1—72 sts.

**Row 10 (and every following even row through 18):** Work in established pat.

**Row 11:** Sl 1, k2tog, k2, [p1, k1] 3 times, C6B, *[p1, k1] 4 times, C6B; rep from *, end [p1, k1] 3 times, p1, k2tog, k4—70 sts.

**Row 13:** Sl 1, k2, ssk, [p1, k1] 3 times, k3, *k3, [p1, k1] 4 times, k3; rep from *, end k3, [p1, k1] 3 times, k2tog, k3—68 sts.

**Row 15:** Sl 1, k2, ssk, [p1, k1] twice, k1, C6B, *[p1, k1] 4 times, C6B; rep from *, end [p1, k1] twice, p1, k2tog, k3—66 sts.

**Row 17:** Sl 1, k2, sl 1, k2tog, psso, k1, Tw5B, *Tw5F, [p1, k1] twice, Tw5B; rep from *, end Tw5F, p1, k3tog, k3—62 sts.

**Row 19:** Sl 1, k2, sl 1, k2tog, psso, k2, [p1, k1] twice *p1, k4, [p1, k1] twice, k3, p1, k1; rep from *, end k2, k3tog, k3—58 sts.

**Row 20:** BO 4 sts, cont in pat—54 sts.

**Row 21:** BO 4 sts, cont in pat—50 sts.

**Rows 22 & 23:** BO 6 sts, cont in pat—38 sts.

BO in pat.

## BELT

With B and larger needles, CO 8 sts. Work in k1, p1 rib until piece measures 45"/114cm.

BO.

## FINISHING

Block the pieces.

Fold ribbed top edge of front and back in half to WS and sew in place, leaving side edges of back edge open to create a casing for belt. Sew side seams.

### TUBULAR BORDER

With B and smaller needles, CO 4 sts. Starting at left side of the flap, *pick up 1 st from edge of the purse and slide all sts to the other end of needle, k3, k2tog; rep from * around flap and then side seams of purse.

BO.

Weave in ends. Line purse if desired.

Insert belt through casing along top back edge. Fold one end of belt over by approx 1"/2.5cm, insert both D-rings and secure.

### CLOSURE TIES

With 2 strands of A and crochet hook, crochet a 4"/10cm long chain starting at center of flap. Fasten off.

Close flap and make another 4"/10cm long chain on front of purse, aligned with 1st tie. Fasten off.

**V**ery functional and very fashionable.
Wear it as a belt to make a statement and
let your hands be free!

# motorcycle gloves

**These gloves are a treat for your hands,** as they're knit in soft silk-and-bamboo yarn. Make them in a dazzling color and they will add a little edge to your look.

SKILL LEVEL
**Advanced**

FINISHED MEASUREMENTS
**6½"/17cm in circumference, not stretched**

YOU WILL NEED

**Lorna's Laces Pearl** (51% silk, 49% bamboo; 3.5oz/100g = 215yd/197m): 1 skein Brick #38ns—approx 215yd/197m of DK weight yarn; **(3)**

**Knitting needles:** 3.5mm (size 4 U.S.) set of 5 dpns *or size to obtain gauge*

**Crochet hook:** 2.75mm (size C-2 U.S.)

**Tapestry needle**

**2 small buttons**

## GAUGE

22 sts and 32 rows = 4"/10cm in St st

*Always take time to check your gauge.*

## SPECIAL ABBREVIATIONS

**MM:** Move marker

# instructions

## RIGHT GLOVE

**NOTE:** *Slip 1st st of every row.*

CO 32 sts.

**Row 1 (WS):** Purl.

**Row 2:** Knit.

**Row 3:** Purl.

**Row 4:** Sl 1, k2tog, knit to last 3 sts, ssk, k1—30 sts.

**Row 5:** Purl.

**Row 6:** Knit.

**Row 7:** Purl.

**Row 8:** Rep row 4—28 sts.

**Row 9:** Purl.

**Row 10:** Rep row 4—26 sts.

**Row 11:** Purl.

**Row 12:** Rep row 4—24 sts.

**Row 13:** Purl.

**Row 14:** Knit.

**Row 15:** Purl.

**Row 16:** Sl 1, M1, knit to last st, M1, k1—26 sts.

**Row 17:** Purl.

**Row 18:** Rep row 16—28 sts.

**Row 19:** Purl to end, CO 2 sts—30 sts.

**Row 20:** Knit to end, CO 2 sts—32 sts.

**Row 21:** Purl to end, CO 2—34 sts.

**Row 22:** Knit to end, CO 1 st, PM and join in rnd—35 sts.

**START THUMB GUSSET SHAPING:**

**Rnd 1 (and every odd rnd):** Knit even.

**Rnd 2:** K8, PM, M1, k1, M1, PM, work to end—37 sts.

**Rnd 4 (and every even rnd):** Knit to 1st gusset marker, MM, M1, knit to 2nd marker, M1, knit to end.

Rep last 2 rnds until there are 15 sts bet the 2 markers.

Knit 1 rnd.

**Next rnd:** Work to 1st marker, remove marker, slip next 15 sts on a piece of waste yarn.

CO 3 sts over the gap, PM and join in rnd for palm. Remove other marker—37 sts. Work even in St st for ½"/1cm, then divide for fingers as foll:

### FINGER #1 (PINKY):

Knit to marker, k15, put next 7 sts on a piece of waste yarn, CO 1 st and join rem sts in a rnd, PM—31 sts. Work even for 3 more rnds, then divide for the next finger.

### FINGER #2:

Knit to marker, k10, put next 10 sts on a piece of waste yarn.

CO 1 st and join rem sts in a rnd, PM , k5—22 sts.

### FINGER #3:

Slide last 11 sts onto a piece of waste yarn.

### FINGER #4:

Work rem 11 sts as foll:

Co 1 st, PM and join in a rnd. Work even until finger measures 2½"/6cm—12 sts.

**Next rnd:** [K2tog] twice, k2, [k2tog] twice, k2—8 sts.

Knit next rnd, [k2tog, k2] twice. Cut yarn and pull through rem 6 sts, fasten off and weave in ends.

Go back to Finger #3 sts and divide these 11 sts on dpns. Pick up and knit 1 st from the CO of the other finger, PM—12 sts.

Work in a rnd until finger measures 2½"/6cm.

**Next rnd:** [K2tog] twice, k2, [k2tog] twice, k2—8 sts.

Knit next rnd, [k2tog, k2] twice. Cut yarn and pull through rem 6 sts, fasten off and weave in ends.

Go back to Finger #2 sts and divide these 10 sts on dpns. Pick up and knit 1 st from the CO of the other finger, PM—11 sts.

Work in a rnd until finger measures 2½"/6cm.

**Next rnd:** [K2tog] twice, k2, [k2tog] twice, k1—7 sts.

Knit next rnd, k2tog, knit to end. Cut yarn and pull through rem 6 sts, fasten off and weave in ends.

Go back to Finger #1 sts and divide these 7 sts on dpns. Pick up and knit 1 st from the CO of the other finger, PM—8 sts.

Work in a rnd until finger measures 2"/5cm.

**Next rnd:** [K2tog] 4 times.

Cut yarn and pull through rem 4 sts, fasten off and weave in ends.

Go back to Thumb sts and divide these 15 sts on dpns. Pick up and knit 3 sts from the CO of the other finger, PM—18 sts.

Work 2 rnds. Next rnd, work to 4 sts before marker, k2tog, knit to end.

Work 2 rnds. Next rnd, work to 3 sts before marker, k2tog, knit to end.

**H**ave a motorcycle jacket? Then you need this pair of gloves to complete the look. I prefer them in a silky fabric as a contrast to leather…but really they make a great accessory on their own as well.

Work 2 rnds. Next rnd, work to 2 sts before marker, k2tog, knit to end—15 sts.

Work even until thumb measures 2¼"/6cm.

**Next rnd:** [K2tog] 3 times, k2, [k2tog] 3 times, k1—9 sts.

Knit next rnd, then [k2tog, k1] 3 times. Cut yarn and pull through rem 6 sts, fasten off and weave in ends.

## LEFT GLOVE

Work as for Right Glove to start of thumb gusset shaping.

**START THUMB GUSSET SHAPING:**

**Rnd 1 (and every odd numbered rnd):** Knit.

**Rnd 2:** Knit to last 9 sts, PM, M1, k1, M1, PM, work to end— 37 sts.

**Rnd 4 (and every following even rnd):** Knit to 1st gusset marker, MM, M1, knit to 2nd marker, M1, knit to end.

Rep last 2 rnds until there are 15 sts bet the two markers.

Knit 1 rnd.

**Next rnd:** Work to 1st marker, remove marker, slip next 15 sts on a piece of waste yarn.

CO 3 sts over the gap, PM and join in rnd for the palm. Remove other marker—37 sts. Work even in St st for ½"/1cm, then divide for fingers as for Right Glove.

Finish as for Right Glove.

## FINISHING

With crochet hook, work 22 sc along the CO edge. Ch 4 and join into a button loop at bottom edge of opening. Work 20 sc around opening on front of glove. Fasten off. Weave in ends. Sew button opposite loop.

# motorcycle rib headband

## YOU WILL NEED

**Lorna's Laces Pearl** (51% silk, 49% bamboo; 3.5oz/100g = 215yd/196m): (A) 1 skein Brick #38ns, (B) 1 skein color Pewter #9ns—approx 430yd/392m of DK weight yarn; ⬤5

**Knitting needles:** 3.75mm (size 5 U.S.) 16" circular needle, 5.5mm (size 9 U.S.) 16"/41cm circular needle and 4.5mm (size 7 U.S.) 16"/41cm circular needle *or size to obtain gauge*

## SKILL LEVEL
**Beginner**

## FINISHED MEASUREMENTS
**18"/46cm in circumference (not stretched), 6¾"/17cm wide (unfolded)**

**This headband is a must-have little accessory.** Made in two contrasting colors and knit in a simple rib, it can be worn folded in half, with a different color showing depending on your mood or outfit.

27 sts and 34 rows = 4"/10cm in k1, p1 rib using smallest needles, not stretched

*Always take time to check your gauge.*

# instructions

## HEADBAND

With largest needles and A, CO 120 sts. PM and join in rnd.

Work in k1, p1 rib for ½"/1cm.

Change to medium size needles and cont in rib for ¾"/2cm more.

Change to smallest needles and cont in rib until piece measures 3½"/9cm from beg.

Maintaining st pat, work 1 rnd in B, 2 rnds in A, 2 rnds in B and 1 rnd in A. Change to B and work even for 1½"/4cm more.

Change to medium size needles and cont in rib for ¾"/2cm more.

Change to largest needles and cont in rib for ½"/1cm more.

BO loosely in pat.

## FINISHING

Weave in ends. Fold in half to wear.

**W**ear it as a headband or perhaps as a cowl, which is quite a popular way of styling it around the neck.

# airy
# smocking
# scarf

**At first glance this piece appears to be very fancy and textural,** but it's easy to create this visually interesting accessory.

## YOU WILL NEED

Blue Sky Alpacas Brushed Suri
(67% baby suri alpaca,
22% merino, 11% bamboo;
1.75oz/50g = 142yd/130m):
3 skeins, color Snow Cone
#908—approx 426yd/390m
of worsted weight yarn; ( 4 )

Small amount of waste yarn
in a contrasting color

Knitting needles: 6mm (size 10
U.S.) *or size to obtain gauge*

Tapestry needle

## SKILL LEVEL
**Easy**

## FINISHED MEASUREMENTS
**11" x 70"/28cm x 178cm,
after smocking**

## GAUGE

16 sts and 10 rows = 4"/10cm in St st, before smocking
*Always take time to check your gauge.*

# instructions

## SCARF

CO 56 sts.

Work in St st until piece measures 76"/193cm from beg.

BO.

## FINISHING

Weave in ends. Block.

## SMOCKING

### PREPARATION

Mark smocking rows by basting a length of contrasting yarn under knit sts of row 6 and on every following 6th row, ending approx 6 rows from BO edge.

For each "smock," cut a 10"/25cm length of project yarn.

### CREATING THE SMOCKING

Fold 1 length of cut project yarn in half and thread folded end through needle, keeping loop on one side of needle eye.

With RS facing and beg at the 1st st of the 1st marked row, insert needle under the 2nd stitch, *then back up at the 8th st (skipping 6 sts). Bring needle back through loop and tighten in a lark's head knot. Insert needle to WS and weave in ends. Skip 8 sts, insert needle under next st as before and rep from * across. For next row, work a smock centered between smocks of prev row. Rep these two smocking rows for pat.

**C**hoose a "fuzzy" yarn for this scarf, as it will give you both substance and delicacy at the same time. The trick is to make it soft and fluffy…that is why brushed alpaca or mohair yarns would work the best.

# herringbone
# bracelet

**Made with pure silk and leather inserts—** two contrasting elements—this bracelet becomes a statement piece. It gets a feminine touch from the lacing.

SKILL LEVEL
**Advanced**

FINISHED
MEASUREMENTS
**7¼" x 4½"/19cm x 11cm, after blocking**

YOU WILL NEED

**Artyarns Regal Silk** (100% silk; 1.75oz/50g = 163yd/149m): 1 skein, color #272—approx 163yd/149m of light worsted weight yarn; (**3**) (A)

⅛"/3mm leather lace, 5yds/6m in color black (B)

**Knitting needles:** 3.75mm (size 5 U.S.) *or size to obtain gauge*

**Crochet hook:** 3.75mm (size F-5 U.S.)

**Cable needle**

**Tapestry needle**

## GAUGE

36 sts and 38 rows = 4"/10cm in Herringbone pat
*Always take time to check your gauge.*

## SPECIAL ABBREVIATIONS

**C6B (cable 6 sts back):** Slip 3 sts to cn and hold in back of work, k3, k3 from cn.

**C6F (cable 6 sts front):** Slip 3 sts to cn and hold in front of work, k3, k3 from cn.

## PATTERN STITCHES

### HERRINGBONE

*(Multiple of 36 + 28)*

**Row 1 (RS):** K2, C6B, [k3, C6B] 2 times, *k3, C6F, [k3, C6B] 3 times; rep from * across, end k2.

**Row 2 and all WS rows:** Purl.

**Row 3:** K8, C6B, k3, C6B, *[C6F, k3] twice, k3, C6B, k3, C6B; rep from * across, end k5.

**Row 5:** K5, [C6B, k3] twice, *k3, C6F, k3, C6F, [C6B, k3] twice; rep from * across, end k5.

**Row 6:** Purl.

Rep rows 1–6 for pat.

## instructions

## CUFF

CO 66 sts.

**NOTE:** *There are 2 extra edge sts — always slip the first and knit the last st of every row throughout.*

Knit 1 row.

Work center 64 sts in Herringbone pat for 24 rows.

**Leather lace set-up row (next row 1 of pat):** K2, C6B, k3, C6B, k3, C6B with leather insert (knit the last 3 sts of C6B in B, carry A over in the back and continue working in pat), *k3, C6F, [k3, C6B] 3 times; rep from * across, end k2.

Cont working in pat, using A to work sts in A, and B to work sts in B. (On next row 1 of pat, rep leather lace set-up row] twice (total of 3 leather inserts.) BO on row 6 of 3rd lace insert rep as folls: BO 5 sts, *p2tog; BO 3 sts; rep from * across, end BO 4 instead of 3.

## FINISHING

With crochet hook and A, work 40 sc along CO edge. Fasten off. Rep on BO edge. Weave in ends. Block. With B, lace bracelet along the sides.

**A**ll of the bracelets in this book are special for different reasons. I combined silk and leather in this one, which seem to complement one another in an unusual way. I loved this technique when I used it for the Herringbone Purse in *Luxe Knits,* so I thought it would be fun to make as a bracelet.

**Smocking adds flair to this simple knitted clutch.** A bit of leather lace and metal rings create a stylish clasp for a chic evening look.

# smocking
# clutch

## YOU WILL NEED

**Blue Sky Alpacas Alpaca Silk** (50% alpaca, 50% silk; 1.75oz/50g = 146yd/134m): 3 skeins, color Blue #127—approx 438yd/401m of sport weight yarn; **2**

**Small amount of waste yarn in a contrasting color**

**Knitting needles:** 3.75mm (size 5 U.S.) straight needles and set of 2 dpns, 5.5mm (size 9 U.S.) straight needles *or sizes to obtain gauge*

**Tapestry needle**

**Lining fabric** (optional)

**Stiff interfacing** (optional)

**Small crochet hook**

**2 metal rings**, 1"/2.5cm diameter

**Small amount of leather lace**

## SKILL LEVEL
**Advanced**

## FINISHED MEASUREMENTS
**10" x 9"/25cm x 23cm, after smocking**

## GAUGE

20 sts and 26 rows = 4"/10cm in *single* strand in St st, after blocking, using smaller needles

15 sts and 20 rows = 4"/10cm in *double* strand in St st, after blocking, using larger needles

*Always take time to check your gauge.*

# instructions

## FLAP

With smaller needles and a single strand of yarn, CO 56 sts.

**Row 1 (WS):** Purl, CO 4 sts—60 sts.

**Row 2:** Knit, CO 4 sts—64 sts.

**Rows 3 and 4:** Rep rows 1 and 2—72 sts.

**Row 5:** Purl, CO 3 sts—75 sts.

**Row 6:** Knit, CO 3 sts—78 sts.

**Row 7:** Purl, CO 2 sts—80 sts.

**Row 8:** Knit, CO 2 sts—82 sts.

Rep last 2 rows twice more—90 sts.

Work even in St st until piece measures 8½"/22cm.

BO.

Block.

## SMOCKING

### PREPARATION

Mark smocking rows by basting a length of contrasting yarn under knit sts of row 4 and on every following 8th row, for a total of 7 rows.

For each "smock," cut a 10"/25cm length of project yarn.

### CREATING THE SMOCKING

Fold 1 length of cut project yarn in half and thread folded end through needle, keeping loop on one side of needle eye.

With RS facing and beg at the 1st st of 1st marked row, insert needle under 2nd stitch, *then back up at 8th st (skipping 6 sts). Bring needle back through loop and tighten in a lark's head knot. Insert needle to WS and weave in ends. Skip 8 sts, insert needle under next st as before and rep from * across. For next row, work a smock centered between smocks of prev row. Rep these two smocking rows for pat.

## TUBULAR BORDER

With dpns and a single strand of yarn, CO 3 sts. Starting at the BO edge, *pick up 1 st from the edge of the flap and slide all the sts to the other end of the needle, k2, k2tog; rep from * around the flap. BO, weave in ends.

## BODY

With larger needles and a double strand of yarn, CO 47 sts.

**Row 1:** Sl 1, *k1, p1; rep from * across, end k2.

**Row 2:** Sl 1, *p1, k1; rep from * across, end p1, k1.

**Rep last 2 rows 3 more times for Rib pat.**

**Row 9:** Sl 1, *k1, yo, k2tog; rep from * across, end k1.

**Row 10:** Rep row 2.

Work next 7 rows in established Rib pat.

Pick up corresponding st of CO row and k2tog with every stitch on the needle to create a folded hem.

Work even in St st for 8"/20cm.

**Next 2 rows:** BO 6 sts, work even in pat—35 sts.

Work even for 4½"/11cm more.

**Next 2 rows:** CO 6 sts, work even in pat—47 sts.

Work even in St st for 8"/20cm.

Work in Rib pat as before for 8 rows.

**Row 9:** Sl 1, *k1, yo, k2tog; rep from * across, end k1.

**Row 10:** Rep row 2.

Work next 7 rows in established Rib pat.

BO in pat. Fold rib in half and sew in place on WS to form a hem.

## FINISHING

Sew side seams. Sew flap to back of clutch, just below ribbed portion. Weave in ends. If desired, cut a piece of stiff interfacing to fit flap. Line bag, placing interfacing between lining and WS of flap.

## CLOSURE

With crochet hook, join yarn and center bottom of flap and ch 9. Join free end of ch approx 1"/2.5cm from opposite end to form a loop. Adjacent to loop on body of bag, tie a double strand of leather lace. Tie metal rings to lace to weight them. Slip rings through loop to close.

**J**ust for necessary items such as your wallet, keys, and lipstick, this bag is light and easy to carry around.

# STARRY
## NIGHT
### COLLECTION

**SPARKLE LIKE THE STARS WITH PIECES FROM THIS COLLECTION.** Adorn yourself with something unforgettable for a memorable night out.

# lightweight cable wristlets

**Made in dreamy cashmere,**

**these intricate** wristlets are

a must-have accessory item

for a night on the town.

## YOU WILL NEED

**ArtYarns Cashmere 2**
(100% cashmere; 1.75oz/50g
= 255yd/233m): 1 skein, color
#128—approx 255yd/232m of
fingering weight yarn; **1**

**Knitting needles:** 3.75mm
(size 5 U.S.) set of 5 dpns
*or size to obtain gauge*

**Cable needle**

**Tapestry needle**

## SKILL LEVEL
**Advanced**

## FINISHED MEASUREMENTS
**6"/15cm in circumference
(not stretched),
9½"/24cm long**

## GAUGE

32 sts and 28 rows = 4"/10cm in Cable Twist pat
*Always take time to check your gauge.*

## SPECIAL ABBREVIATIONS

**C4B (cable 4 sts back):** Slip 2 sts to cn and hold in back of work, k2, k2 from cn.

**Tw4B (twist 4 sts back):** Slip 2 sts to cn and hold in back of work, k2, p2 from cn.

**Tw4F (twist 4 sts front):** Slip 2 sts to cn and hold in front of work, p2, k2 from cn.

**C4F (cable 4 sts front):** Slip 2 sts to cn and hold in front of work, k2, k2 from cn.

**MM:** Move marker

## PATTERN STITCHES

**CABLE TWIST**

(Multiple of 8)

**Rnds 1, 2, and 4:** *P4, k4; rep from * around.

**Rnd 3:** *P4, C4B; rep from * around.

**Rnds 5–8:** Rep rnds 1–4.

**Rnd 9:** P2, *Tw4B, Tw4F; rep from * around,
end Tw4F, MM to next p st.

**Rnds 10 and 12:** *P4, k4; rep from * around.

**Rnd 11:** *C4F, p4; rep from * around.

**Rnd 13:** P2, *Tw4B, Tw4F, end Tw4F, MM to next purl st.

**Rnds 14 and 15:** Rep rnds 2 and 3.

**Rnd 16:** Rep rnd 2.

Rep rnds 1–16 for pat.

# instructions

## WRISTLETS

(Make 2)

CO 48 sts. PM and join in rnd.

## PICOT BORDER

**Rnds 1–3:** Knit.

**Rnd 4:** *K2tog, yo; rep from * around.

**Rnds 5–7:** Knit.

**Rnd 8:** Pick up corresponding st of CO row and k2tog with every stitch on needle to create a folded hem.

Work rnds 1–16 of Cable Twist pat twice, then work rnds 1–7 once more.

For rest of wristlet, rep pat rnds 1–8 only, beg with rnd 8. *At the same time,* beg thumb gusset shaping as follows:

**Next rnd:** P2, PM, M1, PM, p2, k4, *p4, k4; rep from * around.

Cont in pat, yo after 1st and before 2nd marker on every rnd and purling sts bet markers until there are 17 gusset sts. BO these 17 sts, remove markers and rejoin in rnd. Cont in pat on rem 48 sts for ¾"/2cm more.

### PICOT BORDER

**Next 2 rnds:** Knit.

**Next rnd:** *K2tog, yo; rep from * around.

Knit 2 rnds more. BO. Cut yarn, leaving a long tail for sewing.

## FINISHING

Fold down top border and sew in place on WS. Weave in ends. Block.

These wristlets provide a very delicate and feminine accent to your look. They can complement an outfit with a lot of texture and color in a very simple way.

**The combination of silk and lace-weight** mohair gives these gloves a beautiful drape and an intriguing sheen, the perfect addition to a special evening ensemble.

# long silk gloves

## SKILL LEVEL
**Advanced**

## FINISHED MEASUREMENTS
**6½"/17cm in circumference (not stretched), 18½"/47cm long**

## YOU WILL NEED

**ArtYarns Silk Mohair** (60% super kid mohair, 40% silk; 0.88oz/25g = 312yd/285m): 1 skein, color #250—approx 312yd/285m of lace weight yarn, (0) (A)

**ArtYarns Regal Silk** (100% silk; 1.75oz/50g = 163yd/148m): (B) 1 skein, color #250; (C) 1 skein, color #257; (D) 1 skein, color #184D—approx 489yd/444m of light worsted weight yarn; (3)

**Knitting needles:** 4mm (size 6 U.S) set of 5 dpns, 5mm (size 8 U.S.) sets of 5 dpns, and 6mm (size 10 U.S.) set of dpns *or size to obtain gauge*

**Tapestry needle**

GAUGE

24 sts and 30 rows = 4"/10cm in St st on smallest needles

*Always take time to check your gauge.*

## SPECIAL ABBREVIATIONS

**MM:** move marker

# instructions

## GLOVES

(Make 2)

With largest needles and 1 strand of A, CO 46 sts. PM and join in rnd. Knit 6 rnds.

### START COLOR TRANSITION 1

**Rnd 1:** With 2 strands of A, knit to 18 sts before marker, k2tog, PM, k18, MM, ssk—44 sts. Knit.

**Rnds 2 and 3:** Knit using 1 strand of A.

**Rnds 4 and 5:** Knit using 2 strands of A.

**Rnd 6:** Knit using 1 strand of A.

**Next 6 rnds:** Knit using 2 strands of A.

### START COLOR TRANSITION 2

Change to medium size needles.

**Rnd 1:** With B, knit to 2 sts before 2nd marker, k2tog, work to 1st marker, with 2 strands of A, ssk—42 sts.

**Rnds 2 and 3:** Knit using 2 strands of A.

**Rnds 4 and 5:** Knit using B.

**Rnd 6:** Knit using 2 strands of A.

**Next 10 rnds:** Knit using B.

### START COLOR TRANSITION 3

Change to smallest needles.

**Rnd 1:** With C, knit to 2 sts before 2nd marker, k2tog, work to 1st marker, with B, ssk—40 sts.

**Rnds 2 and 3:** Knit using B.

**Rnds 4 and 5:** Knit using C.

**Rnd 6:** Knit using B.

**Next 12 rnds:** Knit using C.

### START COLOR TRANSITION 4

**Rnd 1:** With D, knit to 2 sts before 2nd marker, k2tog, work to 1st marker, with C, ssk—38 sts.

**Rnds 2 and 3:** Knit using C.

**Rnds 4 and 5:** Knit using D.

**Rnd 6:** Knit using C.

**Next 6 rnds:** Knit using D.

### THUMB GUSSET SHAPING

Work to 2nd marker, M1, k1, M1, PM (marker #3).

Inc 1 st after 2nd and before 3rd markers every other rnd until there are 19 sts bet markers.

Slide these 19 sts on a piece of waste yarn.

CO 3 sts over gap and join in rnd for palm, PM—40 sts. Work even for 1"/2.5cm, then divide for fingers.

### FINGER #1

Knit to marker, k4, put last 11 sts worked onto dpns, CO 3 more sts and join in a rnd (put rem 29 sts on a piece of waste yarn).

Work these 14 sts until finger measures 1¾"/4cm.

**Next rnd:** [Sl 1, k2tog, psso, k4] twice—10 sts.

Knit 1 rnd.

**Next rnd:** [Sl 1, k2tog, psso, k2] twice. Cut yarn and slide yarn through rem 6 sts, fasten off.

### FINGER #2

Slide 5 sts from one side of waste yarn to needles, CO 1 st, slide 5 sts from other side of waste yarn, pick up and knit 3 sts from CO of other finger, PM and join in rnd—14 sts. Work as for Finger #1.

### FINGER #3

Slide 5 sts from one side of waste yarn to needles, CO 1 st, slide 5 sts from other side of waste yarn, pick up and knit 1 st from CO of other finger, PM and join in rnd—12 sts. Work even until finger measures 1¾"/4cm.

**Next rnd:** [Sl 1, k2tog, psso, k3] twice—8 sts.

Knit 1 rnd.

**Next rnd:** [Sl 1, k2tog, psso, k1] twice—4 sts. Cut yarn and slide yarn through rem sts, fasten off.

### FINGER #4

Slide rem 9 sts from waste yarn to needles, pick up and knit 1 st from CO of other finger, PM and join in rnd—10 sts.

Work even until finger measures 1¼"/3cm.

**Next rnd:** [Sl 1, k2tog, psso] 3 times, k1—4 sts. Cut yarn and slide yarn through rem sts, fasten off.

### THUMB

Slide held 19 sts onto needles, pick up and knit 3 sts from side of palm, PM and join in rnd—22 sts.

**Next rnd:** Knit.

**Next rnd:** Sl 1, k2tog, psso, knit to end.

Rep last 2 rnds twice more—16 sts.

Work 10 rnds even.

**Next rnd:** [Sl 1, k2tog, psso, k5] twice—12 sts.

Knit 1 rnd.

**Next rnd:** [Sl 1, k2tog, psso, k3] twice—8 sts.

Knit 1 rnd.

**Next rnd:** [Sl 1, k2tog, psso, k1] twice—4 sts.

Cut yarn and slide yarn through rem sts, fasten off.

## FINISHING

Weave in ends.

These luxurious gloves definitely make a statement. Originally I was planning to make them in a more bold color but then realized that they are quite distinctive in this pale colorway. If you are not afraid to wear them bright and loud, though, definitely do!

# corseted belt

**Knit tightly in a silk yarn, this belt** has enough tension and structure to serve as a corset. Created in panels and laced on the sides, it will be the most outstanding piece of your outfit.

## YOU WILL NEED

**ArtYarns Beaded Pearl and Sequins** (100% silk with glass beads and sequins; 1.75oz/50g = 80yd/73m): 1 skein, color #244—approx 80yd/73m of DK weight yarn; (3) (A)

**ArtYarns Silk Pearl** (100% silk; 1.75oz/50g = 170yd/155m): 1 skein, color #244—approx 170yd/155m of DK weight yarn; (3) (B)

**Knitting needles:** 3.75mm (size 5 U.S.) straight needles *or size to obtain gauge*

**Crochet hook:** 2.25mm (size B-1 U.S.)

**Cable needle**

**Tapestry needle**

**2 yd/2m of leather lace**

## SKILL LEVEL
**Advanced**

## FINISHED MEASUREMENTS
**22"/56cm in circumference (not stretched), 5"/13cm deep**

## GAUGE

22 sts and 36 rows = 4"/10cm in Center Front panel using A

*Always take time to check your gauge.*

## SPECIAL ABBREVIATIONS

**M1p:** Make 1 purl: Increase by twisting and purling bar between the 2 sts of the previous row.

**P2so:** Pass 2 slipped sts over.

# instructions

## BELT

### CENTER FRONT PANEL

With A, CO 44 sts.

**NOTE:** *There are 2 extra edge sts — always slip 1st and knit last st of every row throughout.*

**Row 1 (RS):** Sl 1, M1, [k2, p2] twice, k1, Skp, p1, [k2, p2] 4 times, k2, p1, k2tog, k1, [p2, k2] twice, M1, k1.

**Row 2 and all WS rows:** Purl.

**Row 3:** Sl 1, k1, M1, [k2, p2] twice, k1, Skp, [k2, p2] 4 times, k2, k2tog, k1, [p2, k2] twice, M1, k2.

**Row 5:** Sl 1, k2, M1p, [k2, p2] twice, k2, Skp, [p2, k2] 3 times, p2, k1, k2tog, k1, [p2, k2] twice, M1p, k3.

**Row 7:** Sl 1, k2, p1, M1p, [k2, p2] twice, k1, Skp, [p2, k2] 3 times, p2, k2tog, k1, [p2, k2] twice, M1p, p1, k3.

**Row 9:** Sl 1, k2, p2, M1, [k2, p2] twice, k1, Skp, p1, [k2, p2] twice, k2, p1, k2tog, k1, [p2, k2] twice, M1, p2, k3.

**Row 11:** Sl 1, k2, p2, k1, M1, [k2, p2] twice, k1, Skp, [k2, p2] twice, k2, k2tog, k1, [p2, k2] twice, M1, k1, p2, k3.

**Row 13:** Sl 1, k2, p2, k2, M1p, [k2, p2] twice, k1, Skp, k1, p2, k2, p2, k1, k2tog, k1, [p2, k2] twice, M1p, k2, p2, k3.

**Row 15:** Sl 1, k2, p2, k2, p1, M1p, [k2, p2] twice, k1, Skp, p2, k2, p2, k2tog, k1, [p2, k2] twice, M1p, p1, k2, p2, k3.

**Row 16:** Purl.

Work last 16 rows 3 times more.

BO.

## CENTER BACK PANEL

Work as for Center Front Panel, using B.

## SIDE PANEL

(Make 2)

With B, CO 50 sts.

**Row 1 (WS):** Sl 1, *p1, k1; rep from * across, end k1.

**Rows 2–7:** Rep row 1.

**Row 8:** Sl 1, work 24 sts in rib pat, slip next 2 sts kwise tog, p1, p2so, [k1, p1], end k2.

**Rows 9, 10, and 11:** Knit the knit sts and purl the purl sts.

**Row 12:** Sl 1, work 23, slip next 2 sts kwise tog, p1, p2so, cont in pat to end.

**Rows 13, 14, and 15:** Knit the knit sts and purl the purl sts.

**Row 16:** Sl 1, work 22, slip next 2 sts kwise tog, p1, p2so, cont in pat to end.

**Rows 17, 18, and 19:** Knit the knit sts and purl the purl sts.

**Row 20:** Sl 1, work 21, slip next 2 sts kwise tog, p1, p2so, cont in pat to end.

**Rows 21, 22, and 23:** Knit the knit sts and purl the purl sts.

**Row 24:** Sl 1, work 20, slip next 2 sts kwise tog, p1, p2so, cont in pat to end.

**Rows 25, 26, and 27:** Knit the knit sts and purl the purl sts.

**Row 28:** Sl 1, work 19, slip next 2 sts kwise tog, p1, p2so, cont in pat to end.

Work in Rib pat for 11 more rows.

Then increase as foll:

**Row 12:** Sl 1, work 19, M1p, k1, M1p, work to end.

**Rows 13, 14, and 15:** Knit the knit sts and purl the purl sts.

**Row 16:** Sl 1, work 20, M1p, k1, M1p, work to end.

Work even for 7 more rows.

BO in pat.

## FINISHING

Weave in ends. Align pieces as follows: Side Panel, Center Front Panel, Side Panel, and Center Back Panel. With leather lace, join Side Panels to front with whip-stitch, rep with Back Panel on left side only.

With crochet hook and B, work as follows on open end of Side Panel: Join yarn, ch 4, sl st to form a loop. Rep across, making a total of 12 loops evenly spaced along edge. Rep on open end of Center Back Panel. With A, work a chain 48"/122cm long. Fasten off. Lace through loops to close belt.

**T**his dramatic accessory draws attention to your outfit and emphasizes your waistline. Make it in bright colors if you want to stand out…or choose neutral colors if you want to accentuate the waistline in a less conspicuous way.

# tonal clutch

**This clutch comes alive with an interesting** mix of fibers and weights of yarn. The lacy trim adds an ethereal, delicate effect, perfect for a moonlit night.

## YOU WILL NEED

**ArtYarns Silk Mohair** (60% super kid mohair, 40% silk; 0.88oz/25g = 312yd/285m): 1 skein, color #250—approx 312yd/285m of lace weight yarn; (0) (A)

**ArtYarns Regal Silk** (100% silk; 1.75oz/50g = 163yd/149m): (B) 1 skein, color #231 (quarter strength); (C) 1 skein, color #231 (half strength); (D) 1 skein, color #231—approx 489yd/444m of light worsted weight yarn; (3)

**Knitting needles:** 4mm (size 6 U.S.) straight needles and 5mm (size 8 U.S.) straight needles *or size to obtain gauge*

**Tapestry needle**

**12"/30cm square piece of suede**

SKILL LEVEL:
**Intermediate**

FINISHED MEASUREMENTS
**5" x 11"/13cm x 28cm**

18 sts and 32 rows = 4"/10cm in St st using smaller needles
*Always take time to check your gauge.*

# instructions

## CLUTCH

With larger needles and A, CO 50 sts. Starting with a WS row, work in St st for 7 rows. Cont in St st, change colors as folls: work 1 row B, 2 rows A, 2 rows B, 1 row A.

Change to smaller needles and work even in color B for 20 rows. Work 1 row C, 2 rows B, 2 rows C, 1 row B.

Change to C and work in St st for 20 rows. Work 1 row D, 2 rows C, 2 rows D, 1 row C.

Change to D and work even until piece measures 14"/36cm from beg.

BO.

## FINISHING

Mark 4½"/11cm from BO edge. Fold up and sew side seams. Weave in ends. Block. Trim suede to fit and line the clutch.

**I**f you are going to make a statement, then make it bright and loud…maybe in the same color as your favorite stilettos… and you will have a clutch that becomes more important than your dress. And of course if you are looking for a subtler accessory, make it in a neutral color.

# sideways folded scarf

**Utilizing different textures and weights,** this piece is a perfect example of how a structured fabric can also have beautiful drape. The folded areas create the shape while the fabric in between creates an airy effect.

### SKILL LEVEL
**Intermediate**

### FINISHED MEASUREMENTS
**20" x 100"/51cm x 254cm, after blocking**

## YOU WILL NEED

**Jade Sapphire 8-ply Mongolian Cashmere** (100% cashmere; 1.9oz/54g = 100yd/91m): 7 skeins, color Dreamy Peach #37—approx 700yd/637m of worsted weight yarn; 4 (A)

**Jade Sapphire Silk/Cashmere** (55% silk, 45% cashmere; 1.9oz/54g = 400yd/366m): 2 skeins, color Dreamy Peach #37—approx 800yd/728m of fingering weight yarn; 1 (B)

**Knitting needles:** 6mm (size 10 U.S) 32"/81cm circular needle *or size to obtain gauge*

**Tapestry needle**

10 sts and 3 fold repeats= 4"/10 cm in pat

*Always take time to check your gauge.*

# instructions

## SCARF

With A, CO 270 sts.

*Fold:

**Row 1 (WS):** Purl.

**Row 2:** Knit.

**Rows 3 and 4:** Rep rows 1 and 2.

**Row 5:** Purl.

**Row 6 (RS):** Fold work to WS forming a tube; with B [insert right needle in st on left needle, then in corresponding st on CO edge; knit these 2 sts tog] to end.

### SPACE BETWEEN THE FOLDS

Starting on a WS row, with B work in St st for 6 rows.

Rep from * 9 more times, picking up sts to join subsequent folds from 1st row of A of each section. End by working Fold once more. With A, BO sts after joining last fold.

## FINISHING

Weave in ends. Block to measurements.

This scarf was inspired by the Shawl Sweater included in *Luxe Knits.* The versatility of this piece is wonderful: You can wrap it around and wear it as a shawl; fold it and wear it as a scarf; or even create a hooded look. This design is definitely open for interpretation.

# folded cuff

## YOU WILL NEED

**Jade Sapphire Silk/Cashmere**
(100% cashmere; 1.9oz/55g =
400yd/366m): 1 skein, color
Mahogany #055—approx
400yd/364m of fingering
weight yarn; ⓵

Knitting needles: 3.75mm
(size 5 U.S.) *or size
to obtain gauge*

Tapestry needle

1 yd/1m of leather lace

## SKILL LEVEL
**Intermediate**

## FINISHED MEASUREMENTS
**8" x 2½"/20cm x 6cm**

**Knit using a folded Stockinette-stitch** technique, this bracelet becomes a three-dimensional object that has body, texture, and shape all at the same time.

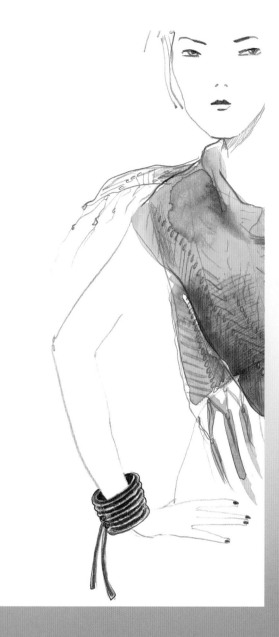

## GAUGE

10 sts and 6 folds = 2"/5cm in Cuff Ridge pat with yarn held double
*Always take time to check your gauge.*

## PATTERN STITCHES

### CUFF RIDGE

Beg with a WS row, work 5 rows in St st, slipping the 1st st of each row.

**Next row (RS):** Fold work to WS forming a tube; [insert right needle in st on left needle, then in corresponding st on CO edge; knit these 2 sts tog] to end (1st ridge complete). *Starting with WS row, work 7 rows in St st.

**Next row (RS):** Fold work to WS forming a tube; [insert right needle in st on left needle, then in corresponding st on CO edge; knit these 2 sts tog] to end (second ridge complete).

Rep from * until desired number of ridges are complete.

# instructions

## CUFF

With yarn held double, CO 40 sts.

Work in Cuff Ridge pat for 8 ridges.

BO.

## FINISHING

Weave in ends. Cut 2 lengths of leather lace, each 25"/64cm. Insert through center ridges on each side of bracelet, pull ends even and tie.

**O**nce again I took one of my favorite techniques from *Luxe Knits* and created a unique accessory, as the densely folded pattern naturally lent itself to creating a cuff. I decided to make it a solid color and quite conservative, but you can choose to make it fun and playful by knitting each fold in different colors.

# crocheted pearl earrings

## YOU WILL NEED

**Claudia Hand Painted Silk Lace**
(100% silk; 3.5oz/100g =
1100yd/1006m): 1 skein,
color undyed natural—
approx 1100yd/1001m of
lace weight yarn;

**Steel crochet hook:** 2.1mm
(size 3 U.S.)

**Beads:** 32 small pearls,
12 medium pearls, 2 large pearls

**Sewing needle**

**2 earring wires**

## SKILL LEVEL
**Advanced**

## FINISHED MEASUREMENTS
**1⅛"/4cm x 1¼"/3cm**

**Starting with a set of pre-strung pearls** and delicate silk lace yarn, these crocheted earrings make a beautiful piece of jewelry. Paired with the matching necklace on page 128, they form a very feminine and almost antique-looking set.

Gauge is not essential for this project.

# instructions

## EARRING

(Make 2)

String 16 small beads, then 6 medium beads on yarn.

Ch 7, join in a rnd with a slip st. Rest of project is worked back and forth in rows.

**Row 1:** 7 sc, ch 2, turn.

**Row 2 (RS):** *Dc, bring a medium bead up in place, keeping bead to RS work 2 dc in next sc, bring up a bead; rep from * to last st, dc in last sc, ch 2, turn—10 dc (6 beads total).

**Row 3:** Dc in 1st 2 dc, dc twice in next dc, dc in next 4 dc, dc twice in next dc, dc in last 2 dc, ch 3, turn—12 dc.

**Row 4:** Sliding a small bead in place after every st, tr in next 2 dc, tr twice in next dc, tr in next 2 dc, tr twice in next 2 dc, tr in next 2 dc, tr twice in next dc, tr in last 2 dc—16 tr.

**Row 5:** *Ch 3, join with sl st (picot made); rep from * across. Fasten off.

## FINISHING

Attach a large pearl to the top of earring. Block.

Attach the hook above the large pearl. Weave in ends.

These earrings look very refined when worn as a set with the necklace. But if you are looking to tone it down a bit, wear only the earrings and you will look a bit more casual right away.

# crocheted pearl necklace

## YOU WILL NEED

**Claudia Hand Painted Silk Lace** (100% silk; 3.5oz/100g = 1100yd/1006m): 1 skein, color undyed natural— approx 1100yd/1006m of lace weight yarn;

**Steel crochet hook:** 2.1mm (size 3 U.S.)

**Beads:** 24 small pearls and 9 medium pearls (color A), 60 small pearls and 16 medium pearls (color B), 1 large pearl

**Sewing needle**

**Lobster claw clasp**

## SKILL LEVEL
**Advanced**

## FINISHED MEASUREMENTS
**17½"/44cm long**
**1¾"/4cm x 1¼"/3cm (largest medallion)**

**A combination of white silk yarn,** tonal pearls in different sizes, and a lacy crochet pattern make this necklace a great showpiece.

Gauge is not essential for this project.

# instructions

### LARGE CENTER MEDALLION

(Make 1)

String 22 small A beads, then 7 medium A beads on yarn.

Ch 9, join in a rnd with sl st. Rest of piece is worked back and forth in rows.

**Row 1:** 9 sc, ch 2, turn.

**Row 2 (RS):** *Dc, bring a medium bead up in place, keeping bead to RS work 2 dc in next sc, bring up a bead; rep from * to last 2 sts, 2 dc in next dc, dc, ch 2, turn—13 dc (7 beads total).

**Row 3:** Dc in 1st 2 dc, dc twice in next dc, dc in next 2 dc, dc twice in next 3 dc, dc in next 2 dc, dc twice in next dc, dc in next 2 dc, ch 3, turn—18 dc.

**Row 4:** Sliding a small bead in place after every st, *[tr in next 2 dc, tr twice in next dc] twice, tr in next 6 dc, [tr twice in next dc, tr in next 2 dc]—22 tr.

**Row 5:** *Ch 3, join with sl st (picot made); rep from * across. Fasten off.

#### FINISHING

Attach a large pearl to the top of the medallion. Block. Weave in ends.

### MEDIUM SIDE MEDALLION

(Make 2)

String 20 small B beads, then 7 medium B beads on yarn.

Work as for Large Medallion through end of row 3, except work in sc throughout.

**Row 4:** Sliding a small bead in place after every st, *dc in next 5 sc, dc twice in next sc, dc in next 6 sc, dc twice in next sc, dc in last 5 sc—20 dc.

**Row 5:** Work as for Large Medallion.

#### FINISHING

Work as for Large Medallion, attaching a medium A bead to top.

## SMALL SIDE MEDALLION

(Make 2)

String 10 small B beads on yarn.

Ch 5, join in a rnd with sl st. Rest of piece is worked back and forth in rows.

**Row 1:** 5 sc, ch 2, turn.

**Row 2:** Sc, 2 sc in next sc, sc, 2 sc in next sc, sc—7 sc.

**Row 3 (RS):** *Sc, bring a bead up in place, keeping bead to RS work [sc, bring up bead, sc] in next sc, bring up a bead; rep from * to last st, sc and bring up 1 more bead, ch 2, turn—10 sc (10 beads total).

**Row 4:** Rep row 5 of Large Medallion.

### FINISHING

Work as for Large Medallion, joining a medium B bead at top.

## EXTRA SMALL MEDALLION

(Make 2)

Ch 5, join in a rnd with sl st. Rest of piece is worked back and forth in rows.

**Row 1:** 5 sc, ch 2, turn.

**Row 2:** Sc 1, [sc twice in next sc] 3 times, end with sc in last sc, ch 2, turn—8 sc.

**Row 3:** Rep row 5 of Large Medallion.

### FINISHING

Work as for Large Medallion, joining a small A bead at top.

## ASSEMBLY

Ch 22, pick up and sc through top of Extra Small Medallion, ch 2, pick up and sc through top of Small Side Medallion, ch 2, pick up and sc through top of Medium Side Medallion, ch 2, pick up and sc through top of Large Center Medallion, ch 2, pick up and sc through top of Medium Side Medallion, ch 2, pick up and sc through top of Small Side Medallion, ch 2, pick up and sc through top of Extra Small Medallion, ch 22 sts. Fasten off. Add clasp. Block as needed.

**N**ecklaces like this are usually great with a simple single-color outfit. Even though it's subtle, the necklace will give your look a sophisticated touch.

# knitting abbreviations

| ABBR | DESCRIPTION | ABBR | DESCRIPTION | ABBR | DESCRIPTION |
|------|-------------|------|-------------|------|-------------|
| [ ] | work instructions within brackets as many times as directed | k2tog | knit 2 stitches together | sk | skip |
| ( ) | work instructions within parentheses as many times as directed | LH | left hand | skp | slip, knit, pass stitch over—one stitch decreased |
| * * | repeat instructions following the asterisks as directed | lp(s) | loop(s) | sk2p | slip 1, knit 2 together, pass slip stitch over the knit 2 together; 2 stiches have been decreased |
| * | repeat instructions following the single asterisk as directed | m | meter(s) | sl | slip |
| " | inches | MC | main color | sl st | slip stitch(es) |
| alt | alternate | mm | millimeter(s) | sl1k | slip 1 knitwise |
| approx | approximately | M1 | make 1 stitch | sl1p | slip 1 purlwise |
| beg | begin/beginning | M1 p-st | make 1 purl stitch | ss | slip stitch (Canadian) |
| bet | between | oz | ounce(s) | ssk | slip, slip, knit these 2 stitches together—a decrease |
| BO | bind off | p or P | purl | sssk | slip, slip, slip, knit 3 stitches together |
| CC | contrasting color | pat(s) or patt | patterns | st(s) | stitch(es) |
| cm | centimeter(s) | PM | place marker | St st | stockinette stitch/stocking stitch |
| cn | cable needle | pop | popcorn | tbl | through back loop |
| CO | cast on | prev | previous | tog | together |
| cont | continue | psso | pass slipped stitch over | WS | wrong side |
| dec | decrease/decreases/decreasing | pwise | purlwise | wyib | with yarn in back |
| dpn | double pointed needle(s) | p2tog | purl 2 stitches together | wyif | with yarn in front |
| fl | front loop(s) | rem | remain/remaining | yd(s) | yard(s) |
| foll | follow/follows/following | rep | repeat(s) | yfwd | yarn forward |
| g | gram | rev St st | reverse stockinette stitch | yo | yarn over |
| inc | increase/increases/increasing | RH | right hand | yon | yarn over needle |
| k or K | knit | rnd(s) | round(s) | yrn | yarn around needle |
| kwise | knitwise | RS | right side | | |

## knitting needle size chart

| METRIC (MM) | US | UK/CANADIAN | METRIC (MM) | US | UK/CANADIAN |
|-------------|-----|-------------|-------------|-----|-------------|
| 2.0 | 0 | 14 | 6.0 | 10 | 4 |
| 2.25 | 1 | 13 | 6.5 | 10½ | 3 |
| 2.75 | 2 | 12 | 7.0 | — | 2 |
| 3.0 | — | 11 | 7.5 | — | 1 |
| 3.25 | 3 | 10 | 8.0 | 11 | 0 |
| 3.5 | 4 | — | 9.0 | 13 | 00 |
| 3.75 | 5 | 9 | 10.0 | 15 | 000 |
| 4.0 | 6 | 8 | 12.0 | 17 | — |
| 4.5 | 7 | 7 | 16.0 | 19 | — |
| 5.0 | | 6 | 19.0 | 35 | — |
| 5.5 | 9 | 5 | 25.0 | 50 | — |

## crochet hook size chart

| YARN HOOKS | | STEEL HOOKS | |
|------------|-------------|-------------|-------------|
| US SIZE | METRIC (MM) | US SIZE | METRIC (MM) |
| B-1 | 2.25 | 00 | 3.50 |
| C-2 | 2.75 | 0 | 3.25 |
| D-3 | 3.25 | 1 | 2.75 |
| E-4 | 3.50 | 2 | 2.25 |
| F-5 | 3.75 | 3 | 2.10 |
| G-6 | 4.00 | 4 | 2.00 |
| 7 | 4.50 | 5 | 1.90 |
| H-8 | 5.00 | 6 | 1.80 |
| I-9 | 5.50 | 7 | 1.65 |
| J-10 | 6.00 | 8 | 1.50 |
| K-10½ | 6.50 | 9 | 1.40 |
| L-11 | 8.00 | 10 | 1.30 |
| M/N-13 | 9.00 | 11 | 1.10 |
| N/P-15 | 10.00 | 12 | 1.00 |
| | | 13 | 0.85 |

# crochet abbreviations

| ABBR | DESCRIPTION | ABBR | DESCRIPTION | ABBR | DESCRIPTION |
|---|---|---|---|---|---|
| [ ] | work instructions within brackets as many times as directed | dc2tog | double crochet 2 stitches together | p | picot |
| ( ) | work instructions within parentheses as many times as directed | dec | decrease/decreases/decreasing | pat(s) or patt | patterns |
| * * | repeat instructions between asterisks as many times as directed or repeat from a given set of instructions | dtr | double treble | PM | place marker |
| * | repeat instructions following the single asterisk as directed | fl | front loop(s) | pop | popcorn |
| " | inches | foll | follow/follows/following | prev | previous |
| alt | alternate | FP | front post | rem | remain/remaining |
| approx | approximately | FPdc | front post double crochet | rep | repeat(s) |
| beg | beginning | FPsc | front post single crochet | rnd(s) | round(s) |
| bet | between | FPtr | front post treble crochet | RS | right side |
| BL | back loop(s) | fl | front loop(s) | sc | single crochet |
| bo | bobble | foll | follow/follows/following | sc2tog | single crochet 2 stitches together |
| BP | back post | FP | front post | sk | skip |
| BPdc | back post double crochet | FPdc | front post double crochet | sl st | slip stitch |
| BPsc | back post single crochet | FPsc | front post single crochet | sp(s) | space(s) |
| BPtr | back post treble crochet | FPtr | front post treble crochet | st(s) | stitch(es) |
| CA | color A | g | grams | tbl | through back loop |
| CB | color B | hdc | half double crochet | tch | turning chain |
| CC | contrasting color | inc | increase/increases/increasing | tog | together |
| ch | chain stitch | invdec | invisible decrease | tr | treble crochet |
| ch- | refers to chain or space previously made; e.g., ch-1 space | lp(s) | loop(s) | trtr | triple treble crochet |
| ch-sp | chain space | m | meters | WS | wrong side |
| CL | cluster | MC | main color | yd(s) | yard(s) |
| cm | centimeter(s) | mm | millimeter(s) | yo | yarn over |
| cont | continue | mr | make ring | yoh | yarn over hook |
| dc | double crochet | oz | ounce(s) | | |

| YARN WEIGHT SYMBOL & CATEGORY NAMES |  lace |  super fine |  fine |  light |  medium |  bulky |  super bulky |
|---|---|---|---|---|---|---|---|
| TYPE OF YARNS IN CATEGORY | Fingering 10-count crochet thread | Sock, Fingering, Baby | Sport, Baby | DK, Light Worsted | Worsted, Afghan, Aran | Chunky, Craft, Rug | Bulky, Roving |

*Source: Craft Yarn Council of America's www.YarnStandards.com*

# index

# about the author

A native Lithuanian and a recent graduate from Parsons The New School for Design, Laura Zukaite is happily pursuing her career as a sweater designer in New York City. *Luxe Knits: The Accessories* is the second book based on Laura's design philosophy; her first, *Luxe Knits* (Lark Books, 2009) features wearables made with exceptional yarns.

# acknowledgments

Many thanks to my mother, **Angelina,** an amazing knitter, for her remarkable help in making the pieces for this book.

Biggest thanks to **my family, all my friends,** and **the Sticks & Strings crew** for all the moral support I've been given!

Special thanks also to **ArtYarns, Blue Sky Alpacas, Claudia Hand Painted Yarns, Jade Sapphire,** and **Lorna's Laces** for providing all of the beautiful yarns for this book. It was a wonderful experience working with your yarns.

Many thanks to the team at **Lark Books,** including my editor, **Valerie Shrader,** and my art director, **Dana Irwin.**

And thank you **Cathrine Westergaard** for your beautiful photography.

**It's all on www.larkbooks.com**

Got an idea for a book?
Read our book proposal guidelines and contact us.

Want to show off your work?
Browse current calls for entries.

Want to know what new and exciting books we're working on?
Sign up for our free e-newsletter.

Feeling crafty?
Find free, downloadable project directions on the site.

Interested in learning more about the authors, designers & editors who create Lark books?